The Spirit of Achievement

Articles, Essays, Speeches

Jacqueline Miller Bachar

Edited by Greg Bachar

The Spirit of Achievement

Articles, Essays, Speeches

Jacqueline Miller Bachar

Edited by Greg Bachar

Rowhouse Press

Books by Jacqueline Miller Bachar

Life on the Ohio Frontier: A Collection of Letters
From Mary Lott to Deacon John Phillips 1826-1846

Poetry in the Garden
(Anthology of California Women Poets)

An Exploration of Boundaries:
Art Therapy, Art Education, Psychotherapy

Images of Mother: A Memoir Journal

La Fête de la Vie (Stories & Poems)

Acknowledgments

The articles and profiles about the following people and topics contained in this edition were first published in *PV Style Magazine*: Buddy Ebsen; Holiday Magic; Eddy Hartenstein; Diane Bartz; Don Lynch and Ken Marschall; Chef Serge Burckel; The Empty Saddle Club; David Benoit; Light & Color; Reinhold Ullrich M.D.; Lowell H. Greenberg; Randy Puckett; Scott Ward; Aquarium of the Pacific; Summer Weekend Getaway; John Koenig; Fall Garden; Gerhard Moser; Jacky Glass; Gerald Marcil; Kei Benoit; Claudia Krikorian; Dorothy Lay; State Senator Betty Karnette; Linda DiLeva-Cooper; Nadine Camden-Kirkpatrick; Uta Graf-Apostol; Reverend Marlene Laughlin; Mildred Sokolski Marx; Janice Bryant Howroyd; Julie Heinsheimer; Jan Napolitan; De De Hicks; Jane Moe; Karen Mabli; Woon Lee; Susie Beall.

The following articles were first published in *Palos Verdes Review*: 36th Annual Rolling Hills Estates Celebration; Associates Hold Sunset & Sand Party at the Beach Club; Yule Parlor Parade, The Burnham Residence; P.V. Women's Club Tea Guests Are Tickled Pink; CAP & Norris Theater Celebrate 10th Anniversary; Art for Fun(d)s Sake; Las Ayudas Holiday Preview; Western Hoedown in Malaga Cove Plaza; League of Women Voters Holiday Party; New Year's Eve at the Norris Theater; Art Walk Features P.V. Peninsula Artists.

"Resident Explores Family History Through Old Ohio Frontier Letters" was first published by the *Palos Verdes Peninsula News*. "Smooth Holiday Jazz Opens Theater" was first published in the *Desert Sun*. Secrets of Spa Cuisine; Divine Decadence; Starters from A to Z; No Mystery Chicken; The Art of Wedding Cakes; Summer Coolers; Dining with the Peanut Gallery were published in *Next*.

Spirit of Achievement portraits: Diane Reeves.

Cover photo & UN speech photos by Paul Bachar.

CONTENTS

Foreword

After my parents moved the family from New Jersey to Rancho Palos Verdes in 1980, a "Welcome—The Paul Bachar Family" article appeared in the *Palos Verdes Review* that sheds light on some of their activities during their first residency on the Palos Verdes Peninsula.

"They believe in committing time and talent to their community," Virginia Twohy wrote, "and are already involved in activities with the Palos Verdes Community Center Association, the Riviera United Methodist Church, American Association of University Women, and the Community Arts Association."

"Paul is Vice President of the American subsidiary of Thomson CSF, headquartered in Paris, and general manager of the corporation's new West Coast operation in El Segundo. Jackie has a degree in psychology and a master's in art psychotherapy, as well as training in fashion and art design at the Traphagen School of Fashion. She is a registered art therapist and was in private practice in the east, taught seminars, and worked in mental health centers."

My mother decided not to continue her work as an art therapist and channeled her creativity into a new endeavor, Artisans International, which she described as a "unique art resource created to meet specialized architectural and design needs for commercial and residential spaces." Her new company offered "a single resource for American and international artists emphasizing fiber and non-fiber works, including tapestries and wall hangings, sculpture, hand-painted fabrics, and hand-blown glassware."

Artisan International's client list included the French American Chamber of Commerce, Coldwell Banker, the Rose Room Restaurant at the Air-Sheraton Hotel in

Osaka, Japan, Price Waterhouse, the L.A. Design Center, Finley's Jewelers, and residences in Palm Springs, Los Angeles, Laguna, and Aspen. My high school curricular and extracurricular activities were punctuated with a steady stream of artists visiting my mother at the house to deliver their wares. I carried many a heavy piece of fiber art from artists' cars into the house and back to my mother's car for delivery to their final location.

In 1987, my father took a new job at Hughes Aircraft Company. Several months later, he announced that the company had offered him a position in their Brussels, Belgium office. He accepted and my parents lived there from 1988 to 1991. After two and a half years of expatriate life to be explored in another book, my father wrote on August 24, 1990, "I'm still waiting to have final discussions on my position in the Space Group back in L.A. Once that's settled, we'll give the landlord three months' notice and start preparing to return, hopefully by early spring."

"While the overall experience has been enlightening, neither your mother nor I want to deal with being long-term expatriates. It tends to put you in no-man's land and all the expatriates we socialize with seem to be basically waiting for something else to happen, like a move back or change in status of one sort or another. The longer we're away from the U.S., the less chance we have of settling into a community we can identify with. It takes time to build friendships."

My father's January 31, 1991, letter clarified my parents' next move. "I'll be in charge of all international operations for the Space Group, including Europe, South America, and the Pacific Rim," my father wrote. "[This] will mean some travel to some places I've never been but would like to see. Hope not too much, though.

We'll be happy to go home. We'll leave about April 7th *permanently*! We have no idea where we'll end up living."

They settled into a house in Rancho Palos Verdes a month later and my father continued working as an aerospace executive at Hughes Aircraft Company's El Segundo office.

Although she had been away from the South Bay for three years, my mother still knew a lot of people from her previous years in the area, and picked up where she left off with community organization work and writing projects. In 1993, she was named Associate Editor at the *Palos Verdes Review*. The announcement of her appointment described some of her overseas and post-return experiences.

"Jacqueline completed a pre-Doctoral program in Social and Cultural Anthropology at the University of Leuven, Belgium and has an MA in Art Psychotherapy from Goddard College, Vermont. She previously served as Chairman of the Los Angeles Coordinating Council for the US Committee for UNICEF."

"During a three year stay in Belgium, she was Assistant to the President of the International Council of Women, an organization with consultative status to the United Nations. Jacqueline participated in ICW's conference in Lausanne, Switzerland, and through her involvement became acquainted with many women leaders from throughout the world."

"She also served on the Board of Directors as Fundraising Coordinator for a hospice program in Brussels. She was a member of Femmes d'Europe, Women's International Club, American Women's Club, and International Study Group."

"Jacqueline is also proud of the intensive chocolate making and pastry making courses she took at the Ritz

Escoffier Cooking School at the Ritz Hotel in Paris. She is a member of the Palos Verdes Art Center, Palos Verdes Woman's Club (Point Vicente Chapter), National Society Daughters of the American Revolution, and the National Council of Women."

In 1993 and 1994, she sold advertisements for the *Palos Verdes Review*, dropped off copies for distribution at the local Bristol Farms and Brentano's bookstore and, except for two articles about Christmas events and the Palos Verdes Art Walk, wrote mostly short accompaniments to photo stories about community happenings.

After my mother met Lili Miura, the owner of Miura Advertising & Marketing and publisher of *Torrance Magazine* and *Palos Verdes Style Magazine*, she proposed becoming a contributing editor responsible for identifying and writing articles about local people and a column provisionally titled "Woman of Achievement," later revised to "The Spirit of Achievement."

Miura agreed, and from 1995 to 1999, my mother wrote 40 articles and interviews for *PV Style*. She also wrote several short stories, a half dozen poems, published a collection of letters discovered during her family genealogy work that were written by an aunt eight generations removed, *Life on the Ohio Frontier: A Collection of Letters from Mary Lott to Deacon John Phillips, 1826-1846*, and edited and published *Poetry in the Garden,* an anthology of California women poets.

In 1995, she spoke about another relative, Elizabeth Cady Stanton, at the United Nations, and was guest speaker at the Stanton Foundation's 1995 celebration of Stanton's birthday held at the Women's Rights Historical Park in Seneca Falls, N.Y.

She was named to head the International Hospitality Committee (West Coast / Los Angeles) for the National Council of Women USA. In this role, she recruited more members than any other individual known in the history of the NCW, and in 1998, was the first recipient of the Elizabeth Cady Stanton Appreciation Award, presented in New York at the Women of Conscience Award Luncheon.

In addition to these endeavors and other community organization activities and events, she navigated the passing of her father in 1993, the debilitating onset of rheumatoid arthritis, and supporting my father through a multi-year battle with cancer, resulting in remission and a celebratory poem to acknowledge the occasion in 1998.

Following his retirement from Hughes Aircraft Company, my parents decided to move to Palm Desert in 1999, where my mother wrote articles for the *Desert Sun* newspaper and its *Next* magazine, started a chocolate company with my father, served as a board member or volunteer for numerous local organizations, and continued to experiment with writing fiction and poetry.

Her short story based on the passing of her mother, "La Fête de la Vie" ("The Celebration of Life") won 1st place in the Palm Springs Writers Guild Short Story Contest and was published in the September 2000 issue of *Palm Springs Life*.

In 2005, she was diagnosed with cancer and arrived at remission within a year, but my father's cancer returned in 2006 and he passed away in March 2007.

"I have written four books during stressful times of illness," my mother wrote, "my mother's cancer, me with rheumatoid arthritis, Paul's cancer, and my cancer. Isolated and separated from society and normal activity, the mind turns inward. The concentration of the inner self seems to release a productive period of creativity. It is an escape from the real world with all its inherent problems."

Losing the love of her life was not like any other stressful life event. Heavy grief reverberated through the years that followed, but once again my mother applied her "concentration of the inner self" to further endeavors that add up to an accomplished final act.

She was producer and host of *The Jacqueline Bachar Show* in Palm Springs from 2009-2011, featuring international, national, and local authors, people in the arts, and community and charity organizations.

She received a Woman of Distinction in the Arts award 2010 from the National League of Pen Women, Palm Springs, and was awarded a Certificate of Congressional Recognition.

She served on the Board of the Palm Springs Writers Guild and in 2016 organized a highly successful fundraising luncheon at the Omni Rancho las Palmas Resort & Spa featuring writer Kyle Mills.

Even though she wrote poems, short stories, screenplays, and a new speech about Elizabeth Cady Stanton and Mary Lott during this period, the writing output that began as she approached her 60th year in Palos Verdes that continued flowing over ten years evenly split between the ocean and the desert represents an especially crystallized creative peak.

The work in this volume serves as evidence supporting the notion that consistently engaging with one's creative interests is not an endeavor of simply finding time to fit such activities into one's life, but life itself, and the embodiment of the spirit of achievement.

Greg Bachar

Editor's Note

Thanks to Jacqueline Miller Bachar for leaving the adventure of this four-year treasure hunt behind, and thanks to those who contributed to the recovery of her writing life and memory: Lili Miura (Publisher and Editor of *Palos Verdes Style Magazine*), Monique Sugimoto (Palos Verdes Library District), Renee Brown (Palm Springs Historical Society), Mary Ann Moran-Savakinus (Lackawanna Historical Society), Thomas Bray (*Daily Breeze*), Corinne (Archives of the UN Secretariat), Ken Burns (Florentine Films), Diane Reeves, Gloria Allred, Uta Graf-Apostal, Claudia Krikorian, Scott Ward, Steve Kelly/Vericker, Kathy Strong, DeAnn Lubell, David & Vivienne Bromley, Kari Burk, Jeff Watson, Stacey Levine, Emily St. Martin. A special thanks to Steve Fleischman, Kae Hammond, and Mary Lou Green, angels when angels were needed.

The Spirit of Achievement (1996-1999)

Kei Benoit: From East to West with Music
PV Style July/August 1996

The Palos Verdes Estates home of Kei Benoit is an artistic reflection of the woman who lives there. Her love of music and the arts fills her home as it does her life. A unique collection of miniature Asian and western instruments carved of jade that she and her husband David found on a trip to Singapore is displayed in the entry. Beautiful artwork hangs on the walls.

Seated in the living room where the sculpture-like strength and beauty of the Steinway grand piano is the focal point, she was serene and thoughtful when she spoke of her youth in Japan. An only child, she was born in Tokyo, where her father served in the Japanese government as the Secretary to the Minister of the Food and Drug Administration.

"I never dreamed when I visited California with a group of students from my university that I would someday live here," she said as she pointed to her wedding picture. Kei's wedding kimono, decorated with orange and apricot chrysanthemums, was a gift from her parents on her twentieth birthday. David, whom she met on a Hawaiian vacation, is a jazz pianist who grew up in Hermosa Beach and played in clubs throughout the South Bay and Los Angeles.

On the adjoining wall are photographs of the happy couple with various celebrities, including President Reagan. "We were honored and thrilled to be invited to the White House," Kei said, where David performed for the President and Egyptian President Mubarak and guests. Next to the photograph is David's 1988 Grammy award nomination for Best Jazz Fusion Performance, and jazz awards in 1989 and 1990 from Billboard.

Kei, a freelance translator in the multimedia field of software and computer games, is also a pianist. "It was both prestigious and popular to have a piano in your home," she said. "I began at age five but had to stop in high school in order to prepare for the university. Because of the pressures, creativity and independence is often lost. But now, I play all of the time." She has also studied and played the lute for five years. Kei is excited about performing with David during the summer concert series at Malaga Cove library this August.

Kei has come a long way from her upbringing in Japan, where, as an only child, she was raised in the traditional ways of her loving mother. She graduated from Kwanseizaku University in 1981 with a degree in Industrial Sociology, after which she worked for a bank.

and living in Florida, her mother holds a Ph.D. in Language and taught at USC and Occidental. She is an intellectual who believed that her children should learn at an early age through rote and memorization.

Raised in Palos Verdes, one of Claudia's earliest memories is walking almost daily from her home on Via la Selva to the Malaga Cove library with an armful of books. She was a fast learner, and by the time she completed the first grade was doing so well that she was skipped to the fourth grade. She was an honor student, yet her mother continued her strict home schooling based on rigorous formalism.

Even as a child, Claudia understood that this was not the best way to learn. "Children want to please their parents and adults. When l was little and couldn't learn something, it was because I just didn't understand what my mother was trying to get me to memorize, not because I didn't want to learn. In education, we owe the children the ability to find excitement in an explosion of learning. In the Montessori school system, children are motivated to learn," Claudia explains, "but learning must have a purpose and relate to everyday experiences."

Claudia recognizes the positive aspects of her upbringing and its influence on her life. From her parents, she gained "an appreciation of the arts and international culture." Her mother is descended from Napoleon Bonaparte and three beautiful fans from the family decorate the wall of Claudia's living room. The Reynouds, Claudia's maternal grandparents, were both musicians and owned a well-known music school in Paris.

Her father John Avakian, an orthodontist who headed the clinic at USC, invested in real estate and retired when Claudia was ten. This enabled the family to spend two to three months each summer traveling the world. In each place visited, they "lived as the locals did." This exposure had a profound effect on Claudia. The Montessori education method, founded by Italian Maria Montessori, stresses that through the introduction of cultural studies, children comprehend their role in the world and society.

Although Claudia began Loyola Marymount University with a major in Liberal Arts and French, she changed to Theater Arts. Interested in education, she "loved working and learning with children through the arts" and believed in the development of the whole person. Claudia's talents in her new field were recognized and she was offered a scholarship to the Royal Academy of Dramatic Arts in London to study with Laurence Olivier.

She never accepted it because, after graduation, she married her high school sweetheart. Fifteen months later, her daughter Corie was born, who when she was old enough, attended the Newton Street Montessori school, now owned by Claudia. Corie, with whom Claudia is very close, is a second year Ph.D. student at the California School for Professional Psychology in San Diego. She plans a career in the Montessori education system.

Claudia has survived several traumas that might have devastated others but seems to have strengthened her resolve. While in fourth grade, she was in a bad automobile accident with her family and suffered broken ribs and collarbone. Her mother, badly injured, was near death. While her mother recuperated, Claudia lived with family friends for a year. Even then, she remained a year ahead in her studies.

Her father died in 1975, and shortly after that, her first marriage ended. A subsequent twenty-year marriage also ended in divorce. However, Claudia has built upon each negative. As in the Montessori philosophy, she seems to interpret what she has learned from her experiences, finds solutions to the problems, and applies those discoveries.

The little girl of the past in the fancy party dress is now an attractive, successful woman. She is a mother, teacher, administrator, and businesswoman is a wonderful role model to the children she oversees.

She expresses it best when she says work is "not my living, but my love."

Musician Dorothy Lay:
A Story of Americana
Palos Verdes Style, March/April 1997

Once upon a time, there were two Dorothys who lived in a place called Kansas. One sang and danced her way to the magical kingdom of Oz. The other Dorothy, with violin and viola in hand, found her way to the beautiful land of California.

Musician Dorothy Lay's story may be as much a part of Americana as the well-known story of Dorothy in *The Wizard of Oz.*

Sitting in the gracious living room of her Rolling Hills home, Dorothy talks about her beginnings on the vast plains of Kansas. Gazing out her window at the beautiful view, surrounded by her collection of early California art, "Dottie" reminisced about her life.

"My father Denton Rossel's family were wheat farmers and Quakers who lived in a typical plains sod house. On my mother's side were farmers, ministers, and musicians."

It's an interesting juxtaposition to imagine Dottie's ancestors crossing the plains in their "prairie schooner" wagons searching for their destiny while their talented descendent now sails the waters of California in her schooner, the sailboat *Water Music*.

"Although far removed from cultural events, my father's family supported his love of music and helped him to attend Friends University, a Quaker school in Wichita," she explains. "He studied piano, became a public-school music teacher and composer."

At five, Dottie and her family moved to Independence. It was there that they developed their talents as a group: father at the piano, Dottie and her brother Bob on the violin, sister Ellen on the cello. Her mother Marie was a talented soprano, and all were active in their Methodist church.

"This early training provided me with a marvelous background in performing," Dottie explains. A member of the Peninsula Symphony, she plays violin and viola and says playing chamber music with the Lapis String Quartet is her "greatest love." "It is an intimate expression; a conversation with music between equals."

"In an orchestra," she says, "great concentration is necessary since the music will sound good only if the conductor's desires are followed. Somewhat like the military, there is no room for individuality."

What Dottie describes as a turning point in her life occurred at the age of sixteen, when she met seventeen-year-old Allen Lay, now her husband, at a church social. Although the relationship grew serious, there were first other commitments for to fulfill.

As the daughter of a music teacher, Dottie had heard and dreamed of attending Interlochen, a summer music camp in Michigan, but it was beyond the reach of the family. Her dream came true when both parents obtained positions there and took the children with them. Beginning at sixteen, Dottie spent five happy summers at Interlochen, two as a concertmistress.

Although she attended Kansas State College in Pittsburg where the family was living, Dottie transferred to the University of Alabama to continue studies with her violin teacher from Interlachen. While there, she played for two years with the Birmingham Symphony.

Allen was attending the University of Kansas and ready to graduate when "an important decision about marriage had to be made." Although "the family understood that I would obtain a college degree," Dottie dropped out of school.

That was 1956—Allen graduated one day, became a Marine second lieutenant the next, and they married two days later. After basic training, they went to Camp Pendleton and have lived in California ever since.

"It's strange how things happen," Dottie says. "The same year we married, my violin teacher died in the middle of a concert, so if I had stayed in school to study with him, I would have lost my teacher and might have lost Allen."

She never forgot her family's desire for her to have a degree. After Allen finished his military commitment, they moved to the San Fernando Valley, where she acquired a Bachelor of Arts with a major in Performance at what is now Cal State Northridge.

She played in the San Fernando Valley and Burbank Symphonies, taught violin and viola, and directed her church's high school choir. She was also busy raising her two children, John and Katherine.

Like her father, Dottie introduces children to music. She does so as a member of the Peninsula Committee for the Los Angeles Philharmonic and co-chair of the Music Mobile program.

"Via the Music Mobile, our organization takes instruments to South Bay schools and demonstrates them to third grade students," Dottie says.

"This is usually the child's first hands-on experience with instruments and maybe the school's only music program. Their introduction to the sounds of an orchestra is very exciting."

She and Allen, now a partner in a venture capital firm and Mayor pro tem of Rolling Hills, also enjoy the excitement of adventurous travel. An Earth Watch archaeological expedition in Sardinia "was outstanding," Dottie emphasizes, "but we always enjoy returning to Rolling Hills. I can't imagine being anywhere else!"

As Dorothy in *The Wizard of Oz* found her way back to her home in Kansas, Dorothy Lay has found her home here, and both live "happily ever after."

State Senator Betty Karnette, Twenty-Seventh Senatorial District

Palos Verdes Style, May/June 1997

Senator Betty Karnette's philosophy is "always do your best." Since her great-grandmother was a teacher, education and teachers were highly respected, and she was encouraged by her family to do her best and achieve in every possible way. Her emphasis on learning, and the drive to "make things happen," led her on the career path to education, and a subsequent role in public service.

As she explains her legislative measures, Senator Karnette speaks with the clarity of an educator. Except for serving in the State Assembly from 1992-1994, and her current position as State Senator representing the 27th district, she has been teaching in California for 33 years.

Senator Karnette was attending college in Chicago when she met her husband Richard, a literary researcher, now retired. After their marriage and move to California, she earned her bachelor's and master's degrees from California State University at Long Beach.

Married for 38 years, she and her husband have lived in Long Beach for 40 years, where she was a high school math teacher. They have an adult daughter Mary.

A twenty-year member of the California Democratic Party State Central Committee, she served on the Executive Board, was chair of the National Education Association's Democratic Caucus, and served on Vice President Mondale's Conference on Educational Issues. Encouraged by party activists to seek office, she was elected to the State Assembly in 1992.

Senator Karnette maintains the dignity and decorum of a long-time teacher, and her gaze is friendly and direct. When she speaks, it is with a slight Southern accent, a result of her Kentucky upbringing. One imagines she was a favorite teacher of many.

Her love of education and its life-long importance is a predominate factor in her work. "Education is the most important issue," Senator Karnette declares. Senate Bill 600, which she is introducing this year, will require California teachers to have a bachelor's degree and to pass the California Basic Educational Skills test before they can enter the classroom. She also supports childcare, class size reduction, and improvement of facilities.

Betty grew up in the small town of Paducah, Kentucky during the depression. She was the oldest of four siblings and was never treated any differently because she was female. She was never told that girls were unable to do certain things. She learned from her mother Doris, and grandmother Betty—the two strong women in her life—as well as her father Coleman, how to get along with men on equal terms.

Since the men in her family respected women's intelligence and opinions, Senator Karnette grew up, "believing that this was the norm."

She explains, "I was never hesitant to speak out on issues, and in high school, although I was liked by the boys, I was considered too assertive, and I wasn't asked out on dates."

However, the Senator explains, her parents taught her "to be pleasant, to listen to people and to have courage;" all qualities which have helped her over the years in both education and public service.

"What happens to a child in the early years determines future academic success," she explains. She suggests that teachers should receive training in music and the arts to use in the curriculum. "Every culture has a component of art and music appreciation which can be adapted to the classroom, not as a frill, but as an aid to the learning process.

"Although Senator Karnette had a happy childhood, books were not readily available. Her family had a Bible, dictionary, newspapers, and popular magazines. As a result, she recognizes the importance of libraries, and "will continue to support any issue that benefits them."

Her father, a "kind, soft-spoken, considerate man," who drove a truck during the depression, read her the funnies from the newspaper. "I remember thinking-at that very young age how he knew what the comics said." She learned to read at age six and is an avid, daily reader, enjoying murder mysteries in the evening for relaxation.

A person with obvious energy and drive, the Senator emulates her grandmother, "a popular woman," who worked eight-hour days in a shoe factory.

She was never too tired to cook, garden, dance, play the piano, and sing at home and church. The whole family participated, and she believes this added stability and quality to her life.

"We moved around a lot because we didn't own a home, but I always felt secure with my family. To this day, I adapt very easily. No matter where I am or with whom, I get into the flavor of things quickly."

This ability helps, since in her current schedule, she is in Sacramento Monday through Thursday, and in the District Friday through Sunday.

Senator Karnette believes that education, crime. and work are related issues.

She says, "The thing that children and their families must understand is how important education is. Teachers and others need to be mentors because children need all the help they can get to do their best."

"The most important thing I have passed on to my daughter that I learned from my mother," Betty says, "is to always do your best—no matter what."

It appears that this long-time educator and public servant continues to do just that—her best.

Horsewoman Linda DiLeva-Cooper
Facing the Hurdles
PV Style, July/August 1997

Twenty-nine-year-old Physical Education Director Linda DiLeva-Cooper of Rolling Hills Estates got her first horse when she was five—at a garage sale!

It was actually a pony, but her mother Frances couldn't resist her youngest daughter's delight when she saw the pony among the items for sale.

Her perseverance showed at this early age. Although Linda studied ballet and ice-skating like many little girls, "the only thing I loved was riding ponies." She never felt afraid and worked hard attending competitions twice a month.

Her father Lou always shined her boots "for luck." At the age of eight, she won her first competition in the Walk-Trot event at Rolling Hills Estates Equestrian Stable with her second pony, Rumours. Her trainer was Julie Smith, her current trainer.

In 1980 at the age of thirteen, she competed in the Onondarka Medal Finals in Santa Barbara on her horse, Fancy Footwork. The competition was considered quite difficult for this age group. There's a "series of fourteen obstacles to jump, with different angles and different approaches in a rather small arena," Linda explains.

Her trainer Julie had won the same competition at the age of thirteen, so Linda might have felt some pressure. Instead, she followed the advice of her supporters to "do your best." Just like all good story endings, she won." My horse was in top form—just perfect," she says, excited from the memory of the day. "To win the same event, in the same place, at the same age as my trainer, was fantastic!"

Linda continued riding and competing until 1983, and then she did a surprising thing—she quit. She was growing up and wanted to try "new things." She always felt, however, that "something was missing."

In 1989, at the age of twenty-two, she went to the Portuguese Bend National Horse Show, where she saw her former trainer Julie, and "that was it; I was hooked again."

That same year her riding began in earnest. Her perseverance strengthened her resolve to train and excel. In 1992, she married Scott Cooper. Upon returning from her honeymoon, Linda entered the Las Amigas de Los Lomas Horse Show in Rolling Hills Estates.

Riding First Edition, she won in two categories in the Equitation Division. She continued competing, and in 1993, wanting to achieve "at another level," she bought a thoroughbred named Maverick.

Show competition is grueling work, which, in the hands of a rider as Linda looks easy. Although she was already in good shape, she continued to work on her conditioning, and concentrated on training Maverick.

In his first competition in 1994, he showed that he "was brilliant" with "lots of heart. He jumped every obstacle and did everything without hesitation."

They were quite a pair and had a series of successes, including First Place in the L.A.H.S.A Senior Medal Finals at The National Preview Show, and Adult Amateur Hunter Champion-over eighteen at the Portuguese Bend Show. In 1995, she was O.C.H.S.A. Senior Medal Finals Champion, and Reserve Grand Champion, Foxfield Finals. She was Best Adult Rider the same year in the Portuguese Bend Show.

Receiving at least eight major awards in 1996, Linda again won in the Portuguese Bend Show as Best Adult Rider and was also Adult Amateur Hunter Champion. With points accumulated for all competitions that year, Linda became Reserve Grand Champion of the P.H.A Western Region. She placed thirty-second nationally in the U.S. Adult Equitation Ranking by Team Ariat.

She was also Bronze Medalist in the P.H.A. West Equitation Medal Finals at The Oaks. The list of awards continued to grow.

In February of this year, Linda was the Adult Amateur Equitation Champion, over eighteen, at The Paddock Show. On April sixth, she and Maverick competed at the L.A. Equestrian Center and everything "seemed fine."

Ten days later, the unthinkable happened. Maverick ate his breakfast as usual, but soon, was in obvious stress. Linda described the scene with great difficulty and emotion.

"Even with the pain he was in, he didn't give up, but managed to walk into the trailer to be transported to the veterinarian hospital."

He died on the way from intestinal stones, a probable genetic condition.

The tragic event, however, had an unusual twist. Just three days before Maverick's death, a horse dealer in Valley Center had telephoned Linda's trainer to tell her about a great horse that he had. Ten days after Maverick died, Linda and her family drove down to meet Durango.

"The minute I saw him, tears rolled down my face. He looked just like a bigger version of Maverick," Linda explained.

On May second, he came home with her. He'll make his debut at the Portuguese Bend Horse Show this September, at Ernie Howlett Park. Linda's dream is to train and enter him in the more difficult Grand Prix.

In the meantime, she'll never forget Maverick. A corral sign behind the house identifies the name of Linda mini-ranch as Maverick Farms.

The little girl that persevered with a new pony has even more reason to work and train hard—for all of them—Durango, Linda, and of course, Maverick.

Nadine Camden-Kirkpatrick:
A Soprano's Melody

PV Style, September/October 1997

Soprano Nadine Camden-Kirkpatrick's Rolling Hills home reflects the "passions" of her life. Central to the living room is her Austrian Bosendorfer grand piano, a "singer's piano." In a predominant spot is an antique victrola with brass horn she found in Vienna but, she laughs, "made in America. We carried it home on the plane and the horn rode in the cockpit with the pilot."

Known professionally as Nadine Camden, she proudly points out her "private domain," a small, charming library filled with leather-bound classics and designed especially for her by her architect son.

A USC graduate, she sings in seven languages and prepares for her performances by "studying the composers" whose works she will perform. Nadine's favorite piece, "Four Last Songs" by Richard Strauss, "brings me to tears. It's the embodiment of what music is all about."

Born and raised in Long Beach, Nadine and attorney husband Robert have three adult sons and two grandchildren who "are my most important passion." Their photographs line the shelf of the family room.

Her philosophy on family life has influenced her entire career. Opera singer Eileen Farrell once told her she had everything it took to be a top professional singer, but that "self-centered, singular purpose was necessary and involved total sacrifice. I wanted to sing, but I didn't want my personal life to suffer."

Nadine decided to do it her way and vowed that she would never be away for more than two weeks at a time, a schedule that she still maintains. She performs about twenty-five times a year and is "doing just what I want to do."

She has appeared in recitals at art houses, salons, libraries, and concert halls around the country. She sang opera in California and Oregon, followed by appearances in Europe. Locally, she has appeared with, among others, the Hollywood Bowl Symphony, South Bay Chamber Orchestra, Los Angeles Civic Light Opera, and Laguna Lyric Opera.

She began performing in the seventh grade when her teacher demonstrated to the class that Nadine could sing the perfect "Ah vowel." She went on to sing the lead in school musicals. After high school, she studied for two years at a small conservatory of music in California, finishing up her general education at a two-year college.

After marriage in the 1960's, she enrolled in USC making sure that her studies fit into the demands of family life. Family again won out when Nadine had the opportunity to sign with a company in Germany as a soloist. "Since it required living there for a season, I decided not to do it when I happily discovered that I was pregnant with my third child."

She has had her share of adventures. In 1985, she went to Russia with the William Hall Choral. She was approached on the street by a man who introduced himself and invited her to dinner. When she declined, he grabbed her arm and tried to drag her away. Laughing at the memory, she described how her "quick thinking fellow chorus members held onto my other arm and won the tug-of-war. We've always wondered if he was KGB."

In 1989, she was invited by the State Department to go on a good will tour of China with her pianist, Manhattan Beach resident Kay Grantham. "It was right after Tiananmen Square, and we were the first Americans that the citizens had seen. Young girls would come up to me and touch my blond hair."

They did five cities in ten days, including a sold-out performance in Beijing. Although the very modern theaters were unheated, "there were always three pianos on stage from which to choose, including the Bosendorfer."

Nadine performed in the Dominican Republic under the direction of Maestro Carlos Piantini, Conductor of the National Symphony. She was the house guest of the maestro and his wife, a daughter of dictator Trujillo. Even though she knew they were always protected by security, it was still disconcerting to Nadine when "I was met at the door by an armed guard and told not to go near the windows."

Much like her favorite character, the Countess in *The Marriage of Figaro,* she has remained dignified and true to her life and life's choices. This charming woman whose voice the *Boston Globe* described in 1996 as "velvety sounding," and "compelling" has managed to pursue her passions—love of music and performance, the classics and history, and love of family—on her own terms.

Uta Graf-Apostol, World Class Ballerina

PV Style November/December 1997

Many little girls long to study ballet and dance the part of the beautiful princess opposite the handsome prince. One such little girl was Uta Graf-Apostol, owner and Director of the Palos Verdes Ballet School, formerly the Palos Verdes Conservatory.

When she was five years old in her hometown of West Berlin, she asked her mother for ballet classes. By the age of eight, she appeared as a pigeon in the Wedding Scene of *Sleeping Beauty*. She "loved the role of Bluebird and dreamed of someday dancing the part."

Years later as a principal dancer with the Hamburg State Opera Ballet, she played the coveted role. Her director was "Peter von Dyk—the Bluebird of my childhood."

Uta's training began at the Charlottenburg School of Ballet, located in West Berlin, but affiliated with the Staatsoper—the Opera House—in East Berlin. Considered "the best in the city," her "very disciplined studies" included all aspects of ballet—dance and theory. Normally, at the age of eighteen, students took a rigorous state examination that included both written and performance. She was only fifteen years old when she passed hers successfully.

Although she was offered a contract by the Berlin Ballet, her parents declined to allow her to tour based on her age. Almost immediately after, however, she began her career with the innovative Hamburg Opera Company in the ranks of the corps de ballet. Later, under the direction of von Dyk, she learned a varied repertoire doing classical ballet as well as "exciting, experimental modern work."

The "most important moment" of her career, however, took place when then guest choreographer of the company, George Balanchine, hand selected Uta to be his principal dancer. Tall, with a strong, athletic body, she was a perfect choice to perform the eighteen to twenty difficult roles under his "patient" direction. Some of the production masterpieces in his repertoire she enjoyed dancing included Bach's *Concerto Barocco,* Tchaikovsky's *Serenade,* and *Orpheus and Eurydice* by Gluck.

"Since Managing Director Liebermann brought to the company the best composers, conductors, singers—the best of everything—it was very exciting," she said.

"I have no one favorite part among them," Uta explains. "Rather, it's the collection of work that gives the dancer special challenges." The company toured major cities, where she performed for French President de Gaulle, the Shah of Iran, and Queen Mother Elizabeth, among others.

Married for thirty years to retired Pan-American World Airways executive Paul Apostol, they have an adult son John. Uta describes their first meeting at a post-performance party in Hamburg as "instant love." They met during the month of October and married the following January. Large, framed photographs, posters, and awards fill their home and document their exciting life.

After sixteen years with the Hamburg company and life in glamorous cities in Europe and the United States, Uta and Paul came to Palos Verdes. Fay Gillette, then owner of the Palos Verdes Conservatory, asked her to teach a class there, where she became choreographer and director. Upon her death this past January, Ms. Gillette left the school to Uta, her friend of seventeen years.

During her long career, Uta recognized "a turning point that came with maturity. Ballet turned me into a different person," she explains. "With experience, I began to feel and interpret the role at a deeper level. Rather than just technique, I drew from more aspects of the character—both pain and natural happiness."

Uta "gives back to her students what she learned." The level of excellence she strives for with her students has led several to be accepted for scholarships in many prestigious companies. Among them is the American School of Ballet, San Francisco Ballet School, Pacific Northwest Seattle Ballet, and the Jaffrey Ballet School.

Although she has lived in many places and met many famous people, her family has been her priority. Uta "loves Palos Verdes and enjoys life in America. My favorite holiday is Thanksgiving. I prepare a fabulous turkey and have an American-Greek-German dinner."

Perhaps the most well-known ballet at holiday time is the *Nutcracker*. Uta has choreographed and produced this for many years—this will be the sixteenth. The production includes many German traditions, and it features selected students and guest performers from companies like the Bolshoi and the Jaffrey.

For many adults, visions of sugar plums are long-lasting memories of their first childhood encounter with ballet and dazzling production. Now, this amazing talent who performed *Agon* for Stravinsky on his eightieth birthday helps students fulfill their fantasies of one day dancing the role of the Princess or the Sugar Plum Fairy. How fortunate Palos Verdes is to have her here.

Reverend Marlene Laughlin,
Minister of The Wayfarers Chapel

PV Style January/February 1998

The Wayfarers Chapel combines the scientific and creative knowledge of its designer Lloyd Wright with the vision of a spiritual sanctuary in a serene natural setting that serves as a respite for weary travelers, or "wayfarers."

The glass building is a physical symbol of the 18th Century scientist and scholar Emanual Swedenborg, whose teachings comprise the foundation of the Swedenborgian Church.

It may be said that Revered Marlene Laughlin, Chapel Minister of the ecumenical Swedenborgian chapel, personifies Swedenborgian thought, the duality of science and religion, reason and nature, intellect and spiritual.

Currently completing her dissertation in pastoral psychology, her academic background in science and education began at Bloomsburg State University in Pennsylvania, where she majored in biology and education.

Listed in *Who's Who in American Colleges and Universities* and with a record of high academic standing, she was nominated for a National Science Foundation Academic Year Grant.

This enabled her to pursue her MS in biology at Ball State University in Muncie, Indiana where she stayed on as an instructor.

Interested in ecology and physiology, she designed a water purification study. Due to the nature of the study, she had to do a count at 3:00 A.M. every day.

"One night," she says, "the lab window had been left open. It was freezing, dark, and lonely. I had a very vivid picture of myself as the weird scientist in a long, white lab coat counting happy, little microbes in the middle of the night and realized how strange it all was. I said to myself-no more!"

That was the beginning of a series of life changes. She taught for a while in Boston, took a sales position with a large pharmaceutical company where she was the first female representative on the east coast, and was briefly married. After her divorce in 1979, Reverend Laughlin began a "spiritual search" that led her to explore several religious alternatives.

Raised by a Quaker father and Presbyterian mother, she spent a "great deal of time in prayer and meditation." From childhood, she had questioned "why is there nature and life and purpose," and so her struggle continued.

Although she was not involved with the church, she "went to a meeting at the Swedenborgian School of Religion in Boston. Swedenborg was a scientist who went through a spiritual awakening and looked at one's own choices, values, and personal responsibility for life's decisions. My search for self and meaning had been solitary and I recognized that I needed a Christian community in which to participate to continue my journey."

As a result, Reverend Laughlin began spiritual counseling with the President of the National Swedenborgian Church.

This was the beginning of what she describes as "the Hound of Heaven lapping at my heels and [it] wouldn't let go." She kept fighting the idea of a spiritual life but took a survey course at the school. The President suggested that she stay for a year, but she left. "I struggled with my decision and two days later I applied to the school and stayed for four years."

Reverend Laughlin's "continuous battle" went on. "God wanted me, but I didn't want to be there. I was naked with God in the depths, and He won. I had been ignoring Him for years and now I was running to life." She spent her last two years of study at the Andover-Newton Theological School completing her Master of Divinity in 1986.

She spent a year in various hospitals in the Boston area interning as a chaplain and spent six years as a minister in a Swedenborgian church in Bridgewater, Massachusetts.

In May 1997, Reverend Laughlin performed a marriage ceremony for her niece in San Clemente and fell in love with California. She "prayed to be here and said, God, whatever you decide, I will do."

The day following her return to Massachusetts, the President of the Church telephoned to ask her to go to Wayfarers Chapel.

She had been in a car accident two years earlier and wasn't easily recovering. Finally diagnosed with rheumatoid arthritis possibly triggered by the accident, she was able to receive proper treatment.

Although she had "contemplated retirement due to her illness," she decided to come to California for an interim period of six weeks in June of this year. She felt "wonderful" and moved permanently on September 15.

Looking out of her office window that faces the ocean and bluffs below, Reverend Laughlin talked about the beauty of the setting and her role within the community. "The Wayfarers Chapel is a setting for spiritual exploration.

It can provide the community the opportunity to be nurtured through workshops, music, and the arts in a relaxing setting. The gardens and the chapel are available for contemplation and are a wonderful retreat."

Besides her chapel work and community outreach, she will fulfill her love of biology and science through her volunteer work. She will work as a docent at Point Vicente Interpretive Center and will act as a guide on the whale watch boats for Cabrillo Museum. This wayfarer has found her purpose, where "the conservation law of matter and energy becomes the crossroads of creation and God."

Mildred Sokolski Marx Celebrates
Her 80th St. Patrick's Day Birthday

PV Style March/April 1998

When Mildred was a little girl, her mother took her to the St. Patrick's Day parade in New York city to celebrate her March 17th birthday.

"All those policemen marching up Fifth Avenue are your friends, and this parade is in your honor," she told the excited child.

Mildred Sokolski Marx, founder of the fundraising entities Hospice Foundation and Peninsula Symphony Friends, may not be given parades these days, but she is the recipient of many honors. Her accomplishments are outweighed only by her charisma and generosity. This St. Patrick's Day, she will celebrate her 80th birthday.

Active in community philanthropy and on the forefront of many other organizations, Mildred is also an astute businesswoman who has had several careers. Executive Director of Hospice from 1986 to 1991, she "saw the need for an immediate increase in funding."

She invited a few dynamic friends to become board members, developed a mailing list with six thousand names, and sent out a letter asking for financial support.

They "raised enough money to pay their nurses something which is always a struggle." That was the beginning of the Hospice Foundation.

Mildred "retired" in 1991 when she and second husband aeronautical engineer Howard Marx married. It wasn't long, however, before she was asked to become Executive Director of the Crail-Johnson Family Foundation in San Pedro, an organization for the health and education of children.

Spending a year there, she helped to arrange financing through Crail-Johnson for the *Partners for Healthy Kids* mobile unit now under the auspices of Little Company of Mary Hospital.

This was followed by two years with the Planned Giving program for Hospice during which Mildred created community events to educate people about the inclusion of Hospice in their estate planning. She has remained active with Hospice and was named "the first honorary lifetime member of the board."

Mildred has cut back on her work because she and Howard travel extensively on vacations and to visit their extended families.

"He's a wonderful Southern gentleman," and their next trip is to Raleigh, North Carolina where Howard, the founder of the Wright Brothers Project, will be keynote speaker at the I.E.E.E, a professional engineering society.

Mildred's early days started in New York where she received a BA in music at Hunter College and an MA in music from Columbia University. Her first marriage to industrial engineer Jerry Sokolski took place the Sunday after Mildred graduated from college in 1939. He passed away in 1984 after a long illness.

She taught music and piano in the public schools in New York and at the beginning of World War II they moved to San Francisco, where their three children were born.

After spending time as a stay-at-home mom, "because that's what you did then," Mildred was asked in 1953 to work with well-known interior designer Ethel Robinson who told her she had a "flair for design."

Jerry moved his family to Palos Verdes in 1963 when he and a partner developed Tahiti Joe Cocktail Mixes. A year later, they built the house designed by Jack Remington in which Mildred still lives with husband Howard.

Mildred was living the "perfect life." She built a very successful interior design business in Palos Verdes, Jerry's new company was doing well, and they were traveling to strange countries collecting exotic art and textiles. After Mildred became ill in 1969, she gave up her business and concentrated on her volunteer work at the Palos Verdes Art Center.

She helped to organize exhibitions in banks and taking on the job of the membership party long before the art center even existed. President of The Circle two years ago, a support group of the art center, she was part of its founding ad hoc committee.

Mildred founded Peninsula Symphony Friends four years ago and was its first President. "Music and the arts give such pleasure to people and yet there's never enough money," so the group was started to support the Peninsula Symphony.

Celebrated by the community many times, Mildred was named Woman of the Year by the Y.W.C.A., Citizen of the Year by the Lion's Club, and Citizen of the Year by the Palos Verdes Chamber of Commerce in 1997.

She is most proud, however, of being given the 1991 Cultural Arts Award by the Jewish Welfare Federation Council of Greater Los Angeles for creating *Celebration - The Jewish Experience.*

Two years ago, Mildred faced a personal crisis when she was diagnosed with breast cancer after a routine mammogram. After successful treatment, she is cancer free and "I feel very confident about it." She is busier than ever.

When asked how she does it all, she smiles and replies. "I've been so lucky. I've traveled all over the world. I have a wonderful family and friends. I am loved—and I love."

Although there will be no birthday parade for her in Palos Verdes, one can be assured that Mildred will have something exciting planned when her children arrive to help her celebrate her special 80th.

It will be a special day for a special woman.

Janice Bryant Howroyd,
Guiding Star of Act I
PV Style, May/June 1998

    Her lavender office is contemporary and home-like. Filled with photos and other memorabilia, a place of prominence is reserved for a framed print of suffragist Elizabeth Cady Stanton and her Women's Declaration of Independence. Written in 1848, it reflects Janice Bryant Howroyd's philosophy of opportunity for all who wish to achieve.

The number one role model, however, for the founder, president and CEO of Act I Personnel Services is her mother Elretha. Born the fourth child of eleven siblings in small-town Tarboro, North Carolina, Ms. Howroyd's mother taught her children that each "had a responsibility to make a difference."

There is no question that Ms. Howroyd, a Rolling Hills resident, has made a difference. Her firm is, according to company literature, the "largest minority/woman-owned employment agency in the Western United States." How she got to this point is much like a Hollywood story. Reluctant to speak of "myself," Ms. Howroyd describes her early childhood as a "product of the civil rights movement." During eleventh grade, she was selected to be the first "integration" for the small-town school. "It was difficult, but it produced good results," she explains. "My father, who was Irish and Cherokee, stressed the importance of education." 'Education is freedom' is what he always emphasized to his family. As a result, after her mother, her "day to day heroes" are her teachers.

She returns to her hometown on a regular basis to visit her mother. She describes the community as "quaint and charming." It was a pre-Civil War "progressive farm in which former slaves moved to one side of town with whites on the other. We have a strong sense of who we were historically," she says. Growing up, she met with the typical prejudices, but Ms. Howroyd describes the local people as "very embracing" of her.

"I have good childhood memories, but I didn't recognize then that "black was beautiful." I learned it through the civil rights movement when we began to mainstream ourselves and I acquired more of a sense of myself.'" Years later, the little girl who didn't know she was beautiful became an in-house model for Chanel in Paris.

She graduated from the University of Maryland, and because of her life's experiences, planned a career in social services. However, soon after her father's death in 1976, she came to California to visit her sister Sandy, one of four siblings now with the firm. Sandy's husband was the head of *Billboard* magazine and Ms. Howroyd was soon working for the publication.

Her sister Sandy tells the story of their being at an industry function at which Johnny Mathis performed. "It was Janice's birthday, so we told Johnny of this. He sang 'Happy Birthday' with the spotlights shining on her. To this day, Janice says it was our way to get her to stay in California."

In 1978, she opened a small office in Beverly Hills from which she placed personnel in the entertainment industry. Now the firm, a full-service personnel company, has 50 offices throughout the continental United States servicing a variety of industries. •

She and husband Bernard Howroyd, owner of employment agency Apple One met at a business conference and married in 1982. They travel often to various parts of the world with their two children Katharyn and Brett but have not yet visited her father's roots in Ireland. Her life is structured around her family and the community and charitable work she does through Act I. Ms. Howroyd's board affiliation includes among others, the Greater Los Angeles African American Chamber of Commerce, International Visitors Council for the City of Los Angeles, Los Angeles Urban League. She is also a Commissioner of the Economic Development Corporation.

She has received numerous honors. In 1994, she was named Black Woman of Achievement, AT&T Entrepreneur of the Year. This month, she received the Anti-Defamation League's Deborah award as "representative of what America should be."

Ms. Howroyd, whose company had revenues of 60 million dollars last year, credits her success as a "gift from God." She returns the gift in financial and other ways. It runs the gamut from full scholarships for deserving students to home hospitality for a 35-member dance troupe from the Philippines.

Invited to the White House for a reception for Russian President Boris Yeltsin, and to a luncheon for Mrs. Yeltsin at the residence of the Vice President, she tells a story that is an example of her unassuming manner.

"At lunch, Mrs. Yeltsin asked what kind of makeup I used," she laughed. "So I told her—no state secrets there." She's truly her mother's daughter who told her "Pride is in the performance, not the performer."

Julie Heinsheimer,
Landscape Designer's Path to Palos Verdes
PV Style, July/August 1998

When Rolling Hills resident Julie Heinsheimer settled into her home in 1968, "there was no garden and no trees except for two lonely olive trees." There was, however, two and a half-overgrown acre of endless possibilities; a house with no heating system; and a time-worn barn with a live-in llama.

Julie and husband Torn had just returned from living in Israel for a year, followed by a four year stay in Paris. Julie studied drawing at Ecole des Beaux Arts and "visited many gardens" while Tom attended the University of Paris.

Tom began work al Aerospace Corporation in El Segundo, and Julie began making their dream home a reality. With no formal training in landscaping or design, Julie laid out the garden, planted trees, and began to remodel the house.

Today, her home and garden are a much-photographed showplace. She is a sought-after landscape designer with Edward Carson Beall, AIA and Associates, an architectural and design firm. She has also been on the Board of Governors of the L.A. County Department of Arboreta and Botanic Gardens for ten years. She is surrounded by and creates beauty.

Julie's childhood, however, was a juxtaposition of beauty and the stark reminders of war. The "little country girl from Texas" went to Japan with her U.S. Army stepfather and her family at the outbreak of the Korean War.

After being wounded in Korea, he was sent to Fukuoka to work in the military receiving hospital. Since there were no Americans in the area other than the patients and personnel in the hospital, ten-year-old Julie volunteered to spend time with the wounded.

"It was a big shock to see them," but she played ping-pong and read to them.

At the same time, she experienced the local culture and learned the language.

"Japan was 'old Japan' and it was a positive experience. It had great beauty. But I knew the memory [of the military hospital] would change my life completely," Julie explains.

"Profiting by the experiences" of the military, the "instability of life" was most difficult. Usually spending a year or less in any given place, she "learned about real family life" when she lived for a time with friends' families.

When two roommates moved to California after high school, Julie joined them. She went to work for General Dynamics where she met Tom, who was working on the Mercury space program. When he later went back to MIT to work on the Apollo program, he invited Julie to join him in Boston.

In 1963, when Tom was asked to go to Israel as a technical expert, he and Julie married in New York City, sailing the next day to Israel. They "experienced local culture, traveled a lot," took flying lessons in WWII canvas covered bi-wings and French lessons at the French Embassy. Then on to France for four years before returning home.

After Julie settled in Rolling Hills, she studied books on landscape design and interior design, joined the South Coast Botanic Gardens and eventually became a board member.

Pregnant with her second child, Jennifer, and mother of 18-month-old Eric, now with the U.S. Army's Golden Knights Skydiving Team, she immersed herself in her subjects.

In 1969, when Jennifer was eleven months old, "a terrible thing happened." They lost their beloved daughter in a tragic crib accident.

"Everything took on its proper perspective after that," Julie says softly as she gazed out at her garden.

A few years later, Julie gave birth to daughter Eden, who now works for the government in Washington D.C. She slowly continued to create her garden and friends began to ask for her help with theirs.

She was developing her career and doing exciting things with Tom, such as balloon racing. She was an attentive supporter when Tom and Malcom Forbes developed the Transatlantic Balloon Project in 1974, and later the Gordon Bennett Balloon Race in 1979. She also "went up several times, but never again!"

She met Ed Beal when their children attended the local Montessori school together, and in 1986 Susie Beal asked her to work on a design project. Only a few months later, Julie learned that she had breast cancer. After successful treatment, she returned to work and is completely cancer-free.

Today she heads the Beall landscape department. She is a well-known landscape designer whose projects range from large estates on the Peninsula to homes in Bel Air and several public facilities. In 1995, she and Bennett Enterprises won first place in the state for the design and installation of a private home in Palos Verdes.

Her garden has been featured in the *Los Angeles Times* and has been photographed by *Sunset Magazine*. Perhaps the greatest compliment occurred when Julie's Japanese gardener of thirty years showed off her garden with pride to his friend visiting from Japan.

Julie has followed many paths to the one in Rolling Hills. "I am doing work that I enjoy," says Julie, "but I am happiest with the success of my children. And most content when Tom and I can sit and enjoy our garden."

Ceramic Artist Jan Napolitan
Finds Her Center

PV Style, September/October 1998

To award winning ceramicist Jan Napolitan, working with clay might be compared to life—"it's a challenge to get it right!"

She has obviously met the challenge, in both the art of life and her chosen field.

In 1997, to recognize her achievement as outgoing president of the Palos Verdes Art Center Board of Directors, the board established the Jan Napolitan Kiln Fund. The financial goal was met, and on October 16, a new gas fired kiln will be dedicated at the center in her honor.

"I had no idea when I took my first class almost twenty-five years ago, that my life would be so filled with my work and the Art Center," Jan said.

It was the Vietnam War, and her business-owner husband Phil was in the Air Force Reserves flying transport planes to Vietnam, so Jan was often alone with her children. When her twin daughters Julie and Jodie started school, she registered for a ceramics class. At the time, there was no physical art center and classes were held wherever space permitted.

"My first classroom was near the old bird farm next to Begonia Farm, and my first creation was a pinch pot. My second," which she displayed, "was clay wrapped around a cardboard cylinder to create the form. I thought it was great!"

A former science and physical education teacher, Jan had drawn and painted regularly, but it was when she began to learn to throw a pot on the wheel that she recognized that the true "challenge of learning ceramics, and creating a three-dimensional form was very difficult."

Jan laughed at the recollection of "having nightmares before and after class," because it was so hard.

She kept going because she was "used to accomplishing things and having a product to show for it." She also learned that centering the piece correctly on the wheel related as much to centering oneself as the clay.

"It's very meditative," Jan explains.

"I found, however, that at the same time, I have to have background noise in order to pull it all together. It's a strange physical and mental control of yourself and the object."

Perhaps it is that ability that helps Jan to focus so fully on the task at hand. Being President of the Art Center board during the term that saw the tragic loss of Executive Director Bev Alpay and now holding the position of Chairman has presented special issues to deal with.

"I don't know what I would have done if I hadn't been able to concentrate on my pots during the difficult times," she says.

Born in Wooster, Ohio, and always "active in service groups," her parents were civic-minded, so her community service was a "natural progression." Watching hawks fly over the wooded area surrounding her contemporary home, Jan smiles reflectively.

"People who know me may not believe it, but I was the high school prom queen."

She was a nominee for homecoming queen as well at the University of Arizona. She graduated in 1961 with a degree in Education.

She has always "enjoyed people and personal relationships" and the "Art Center has helped me to grow and develop strong friendships."

Jan's service to the Art Center has included membership in the Associated, The Business Council, and the Circle. She helped to organize The Third Dimension Group. A founding member of the Artists' Studio Gallery, she is now its director.

Jan looks forward to the time when she can concentrate on creating and exhibiting her sculptural art pieces.

"The functional pieces have been very successful and I'm currently working on the more difficult Chinese-red glazes."

She estimates that through the years, she has probably made about "seven to eight thousand pieces."

Her wares are in various galleries including, of course, the Artists' Studio. She is also a participant every summer in the Malaga Cove Lawn Show and Art for Fun(d)s Sake in October.

A "major accomplishment" is being the first to have her functional work sold through the Bristol Farms chain throughout Southern California.

Jan has never taught a ceramic's class and "never will!" She keeps ceramics just for "myself," and her class day is "inviolate." In her opinion, ceramics was a "crossroads" for her.

"Who knows," Jan states, "I might have become an interior designer."

"Years ago," she explains, "I put the check in my mailbox for an Interior Design class. When I walked back into the house, I received a telephone call about my grandmother's death, and I had to leave immediately. I walked outside and removed the check."

After her return, she registered in the ceramics class and has been a ceramic artist ever since. Jan believes her work was "meant to be."

She describes her art as "meeting every expectation. I learn from my mistakes and keep them out in front of me."

Jan uses her "hammer as quality control, but it's hard to do. It's tough to say goodbye."

Clearly, she can meet the challenge. Jan and her art will be in the center of things for a long time to come.

De De Hicks, Executive Director
of the Volunteer Center:
An Out of the Ordinary Woman

PV Style, November/December 1998

During the holiday season, many individuals give their time and money to help others. In this time of sharing and giving, none stands out more than De De Hicks, Executive Director since 1986 of The Volunteer Center, South Bay/Harbor/Long Beach. Her mantra is "don't let anything be ordinary."

Volunteerism, a major part of De De's life, led to her current position. It also brought her the distinction of being awarded the International Carnation Award, Gamma Phi Beta in 1992. She has also served on the National Board of Volunteer Centers from 1994-1996.

It all started in the small community of Mount Vernon, Iowa. Everything she loves to do today began there. Raised on a farm, De De was active with the 4-H club, which "gave me important leadership skills." Her involvement progressed through college, where she represented "4-H girls" at the state level and continued up to her marriage to now-retired executive Allen Hicks.

"I've always been a people person and love to entertain, which really began after our family moved into a huge old house in town," De De explains. "My father died when he was only 38 years old. I was the oldest of four children, therefore, Mother encouraged me to try anything I wanted to do. Our house became the teen gathering spot, and so I started cooking. Mother guided and encouraged me, and even did the dishes for me," the former homecoming Queen and cheerleader recalls.

Her skills became so good, that McCall's Magazine wrote an article about her called "Born to Cook." After that article and photographs of her Czechoslovakian yeast rolls appeared, she felt "compelled to be a good cook." But her try at Floating Island, a dessert prepared for her new boyfriend Allen and his parents was, she laughs, "a disaster, not at all what it was supposed to be. That brought me back to reality."

De De's design skills have helped to create a unique fashion style that reflects her artistic flair. "That all began with paper dolls," she laughs. "The winters were so bad that to amuse myself, I used to design clothes in which to dress the dolls." Later, through the 4-H club, she learned to sew and made her own clothes.

She attributes her strength in life to those "freezing winters" during which she had to walk to school in below zero weather "being careful not to fall" into the huge snow drifts.

For De De, the trauma of losing her father when a sophomore in high school "was the worst thing in the world to me. I felt after that I could face anything." As a result, her philosophy is that "every worthwhile endeavor in life has an element of fear. It requires something that one hasn't done before, so just do it!"

Her volunteer spirit was also enhanced by the "sense of community" exhibited by the people in her town. "Everyone's talent was acknowledged and used. At harvest time, neighbors went from farm to farm helping each other." Her memory is of tables filled with "wonderful Czech food and of men and women working together."

As a young 4-H member, De De was one of three girls selected to model in the *Farm Journal* magazine. The photo ended up in *Time* magazine with the caption, "To marry well, marry a farmer's daughter."

"To me that was a compliment," she laughs, "because I found the women so inspiring."

De De continues to find inspiration in her current position. The Volunteer Center, which just celebrated its 35th birthday, is one of 500 under the umbrella of the parent organization, the Points of Light Foundation.

Her list of accomplishments is long and varied. De De was delegate to the President's Summit on Volunteerism in 1997. She coordinated the 1993 First Lady of California Outstanding Volunteer Awards. She was named YWCA Woman of the Year in 1986, Palos

Verdes Peninsula Citizen of the Year in 1987, and International Soroptimist Woman of Distinction in 1988.

In 1991, under De De's leadership, the Volunteer Center was awarded the Gloria Deukmejian Founder's Award as number one Volunteer Center in California.

Her "just do it" philosophy has been applied to a number of organizations. She is past president of the Associates of the Palos Verdes Art Center and past president of the Community Association of the Peninsula. She has held board positions in her homeowner's association and church as well as many others.

De De's philosophy is exhibited in her role as a host of a community cable television series, Volunteer Update, founder of Four Circles, an assistance group for orphans, coordinator of Car Care Clinics for Women, found of Legacy, which promotes donor organ transplant education, and board member of Mary and Joseph Retreat House.

As a former food columnist, a mother of four sons, and grandmother of four, she "just does it" in anything but an ordinary way.

"Of Thee I Sing" says Norris Theatre Co-Founder Jane Moe

Palos Verdes Style, January/February 1999

No one sings the Norris Theatre's praises more than Joan Moe of Rolling Hills Estates. She dances and belts out show tunes too. Singing for her supper is something that she does well since she has done more than her share of fundraising and continues to do so. All for the theater—but not just any theater—the Peninsula's very own Norris Theatre.

Former chairman of the Theatre Management Board that she formed, she became involved when it was just an idea in the heart and mind of her late, fellow co-founder Agnes Moss. In 1977, Agnes solicited her participation in the project as founding Vice President of what would be the Community Association of the Peninsula. There were, at the time, many possibilities discussed, including a community hall and youth center, but Joan reminded Agnes that her own personal love was theater.

Sitting in her off-white living room, Joan resembles the quintessential Californian. Although she arrived in California in 1958 and is an "almost native," she was born in small town New Philadelphia, Ohio. She graduated from Northwestern University in 1956 with a B.S in Education and majored in English with a minor in Journalism.

Joan's father Joseph Hurst was the newspaper publisher in town and although she worked in the field for a time, she chose to teach English and Journalism in a secondary school in Ohio.

Joan's father had a quartet and taught her all about harmony singing. As a girl, she made up shows, and was also involved in school projects, but she really got into the theater when she was in college. She did variety shows, sang with a band, and was in chorus and choir.

She met husband Richard Moe after her arrival in California where they lived in the same Westwood apartment building. By this time, Joan was modeling professionally. She had been taken "under the wing" of movie actress Rita LaRoy, who owned a modeling school and asked Joan to teach. Later, she ran the Flair School in North Hollywood, a "finishing school for children of movie people."

After Joan and Dick married in Santa Barbara, they again moved into Westwood. "It was quite a mix of people there then," Joan explains. "People like Roger Moore and Christine Jorgensen, and everyone in between lived in our building."

They moved to Anaheim in 1961 where they spent a year. When his company wanted him to return to Milwaukee, Dick went to work instead for TRW, from which he retired five years ago. The Moes moved to the Peninsula where they've lived in the same house for 35 years, "with many additions and changes."

Joan worked at the Flair school until 1964, then joined the Rolling Hills Estates Women's Club, had two children, and became involved at their schools and at the local Lutheran church. All were venues for her theatrical talents.

Her community activities increased. She became a member of the Parks and Activities Commission from 1971-1973, Past Chairman and member of the Planning Commission from 1973-1982 and has been a travel counselor since 1973.

The theater organization became a crossroads in her life. "In the early days, the hardest part was in convincing people, that [it] was a reality," explains Joan.

Joan's musical talents are showcased with the Prime Time Players. She performed for the first time in the chorus in *Of Thee I Sing*. She has been in several shows including the lead in *Hello Dolly* and *Call Me Madam*. Her favorite was *Anything Goes* because there was "lots of dancing."

Like any theater, amusing things happen. In *Pajama Game,* the scenery "collapsed around her, but they just picked it up and the show went on," she laughs. Her toughest stage feat, however, was in *Anything Goes*. A large stairway behind the set allowing Joan to get to the second level of the set was moved away during the show. She had to "hoist herself along the back sides of the scenery to be able to make her entrance."

Named Palos Verdes Citizen of the Year in 1983, and Torrance Y.W.C.A Woman of the Year in 1990, Joan continues her commitment to the theater. She is a member of the advisory board, does orientation for new members and serves on the Harlyne J. Norris Pavilion fundraising committee of which Dick is the chairman.

"We have to raise a half million dollars each year, and we have the Pavilion," being built across the street, "to raise money for, so next year, I'll be nudging people in the ribs."

Who knows—if you ask her to—she may just sing for you.

Palos Verdes Country Club Golf Club
Women's Champion Karen Mabli
PV Style March/April 1999

"Women's golf is the fastest growing sport for women," according to Karen Mabli, Women's Club Champion at Palos Verdes Country Club. She should know because not only does she compete at the club level, she also plays tournament golf. In addition, she works with youngsters to encourage their participation in the sport.

Raised in Glendora and taught by her late father, she has played golf since she was ten years of age, playing in many local tournaments and winning the eleven years and under Southern California tournament. She reached the semi-finals of the Southern California Junior

Championship during her teens, and at the age of seventeen was ranked 13th nationwide. he was "embarrassed and shy about it," because then, her friends were the cheerleaders, and she was the "athlete, one of the boys."

That changed when in October 1966, while competing in the U. S. Junior National Championship, *Seventeen* magazine selected Karen for their special issue of outstanding teens. She was flown to New York, put up at the Waldorf Astoria, taken to Elizabeth Arden for a makeover followed by her photo shoot. After that, she was considered "one of the girls." At eighteen, no longer considered a junior golfer, she went off to Citrus College where there was no women's golf. After attending the junior college for a year and a half, she left school to become a flight attendant, "the most feminine job that I could think of." While based in New York City, she "quit golf and didn't play again for ten years."

Golf became a part of her life again when after her marriage in 1977 to husband Robert and with his encouragement, she joined Los Verdes Women's Golf Club, played in their tournaments and others such as Long Beach City and Los Angeles City. Then in 1993, Karen entered the U.S. Women's Amateur Championship qualifier held at San Diego Country Club.

It was a true test of her competitive spirit because about 90% of the women were of college age who competed daily on their school golf teams. Karen laughed good-naturedly when she told the story of one young woman who asked if she had ever played in a national tournament before. Karen answered that she had, "in 1968."

The young woman said incredulously, "How old are you anyway?" When Karen told her, the young woman said in amazement, "Gosh, you're older than my mother!" That gave her the strength to try harder. "I told myself I wasn't over the hill and haven't even begun yet!" Unfortunately, she didn't do well enough to qualify, but being around the talented young women inspired her to tell her instructor Randy Peterson "Let's get better." Not only did her golf improve, but the game gave her the incentive to start a company, Premium Marketing Group, dealing in promotional products for corporations.

She started working out of her home with one item, a golf shirt with a logo for clients that developed from her golf contacts. Now she acts as distributor for over four thousand manufacturers, does over a million dollars of sales a year with her product line, and deals with about 300 clients, from individual businesses to Fortune 500 companies.

Karen has been the Palos Verdes Country Club champion each year from 1993 through 1998. She continues to play in local championships and has competed in the California State Amateur Championship and the National Amateur Championship.

Although she has had no wins, she qualified for the U.S. Amateur Championship and the U.S. Mid-Amateur Championship. Soon, she will play in her first U.S. Women's Senior Championship.

"It's the best it's ever been since I've been back in golf. I have wonderful experiences, friendships, and competitions. I plan to continue until I'm too old to compete."

As Karen puts it, "My dad always said don't be a quitter!"

Rolling Hills Country Club Women's Champion Woon Lee

PV Style March/April 1999

Born in Pyongyang, Korea, Rancho Palos Verdes resident Woon Lee didn't take up golf until 1985. By that time, her three children were grown, and she wanted to be able to play with her husband and take golf trips with their friends.

She took lessons at Los Verdes Golf Club along with three women friends and had a ready-made foursome. She joined the Los Verdes Women's Club and obviously was a fast learner because she almost immediately started in competition play.

A grandmother with two grandchildren, Woon recognizes that "golf is a mental as well as physical game," and admits to being "a little nervous" in her first tournament. She finds it "always interesting and fun," and "always different" with many surprises.

She and husband Byong, a retired businessman, have been members at Rolling Hills Country Club since 1986. They married in 1961, the year that Woon graduated from Pyongyang's Ewha Women's University with a degree in Home Economics.

They left Korea in 1974 and moved to Grenada Hills to live with Byong's family. For Woon, the most difficult part of the move was the English language. Even though she studied it all through junior high and high school, "using it every day was harder." She found the rest of life in California pleasant, and with the help of her sister-in-law, things like grocery shopping were "fun."

She and Byong moved to Palos Verdes in 1979 with their children, and Woon spent her time in family activities. She enjoys cooking and prepares mainly Korean dishes, but she does like seafood and steak cooked the American way. She also enjoys Japanese cuisine. Her favorite parts of the golf trips she takes with friends are the social evenings over good meals.

She takes a golf trip twice a year with her husband and their friends. One of her favorites was a trip to Whistler's Resort in Vancouver, Canada. "Golf provides not only a challenge on the course, but offers beauty in the surroundings as well," Woon explains. She plays every day on her trips and has a regular game twice a week at home.

Woon was Women's Club Champion in 1995 and 1998 and has a 13 handicap. The reigning champion must then run the tournament the following year and cannot compete, so Woon will be in charge this April during the competition. However, she will play in other club events including the President's Cup and the Major Guest.

The hiatus enables her to concentrate on another love, singing. She is a mezzo-soprano and member of her high school Alumni Association Choir, whose members will perform in concert at the Wilshire Ebell Theater on Sunday, April 11. More than 100 members from Los Angeles, New York City, Washington, D. C and Seoul, Korea will join to sing, led by their former teacher from Korea.

Woon wishes to attain "more distance" in her golf game, plan another golf trip, perhaps to Kauai, and develop a "fluid swing" like Fred Couples. "I want to play as long as I can. As long as I stay healthy, it's a good life."

As an example, she tells the story of playing golf in Banff while elk were on the course.

"They didn't bother us. They just watched and we played around them."

The Sense and Sensibility
of Interior Designer Susie Beall
PV Style, May/June 1999

What do the military and art have in common? They are the constants in Susie Beall's life. Her father John Riddick, a career Navy man, was stationed with his wife Dorothy in Portsmouth, Virginia when their first daughter, whom they named Susan Merrill, was born. On that day, Susie's mother and astronaut Alan Shepard's wife Louise were hospital roommates. Three more daughters followed along with eighteen moves in twelve years. When it was time for another move, Susie's mother always happily announced to her children, "Girls, we're off on another adventure!"

Growing up, Susie lived in cities like Bethesda, Pensacola, Corpus Christi, and San Diego, where her father retired with Commander rank. She recalls "spending a lot of time with all the girls piled in the family station wagon heading to the new destination with lots of laughing." Susie describes her mother as "very funny which made the moves fun. I guess humor is part of the gene pool," she says. "Because I love to laugh and have a good time."

Susie had to learn to be "self-sustaining, adaptive, and obedient." She also learned to amuse herself and did so through art. "I was very artistic, always sketching and making things," Susie explains. "I never wanted to watch television because I spent the time drawing." All these things sustained her and served her well in later life when she started her career as an interior designer with the firm of Edward Carson Beall and Associates. She returned to school for further study to pass a two-day exam requirement for membership in The American Society of Interior Designers.

Susie, married for twenty years to the firm's owner-architect Ed Beall, has stopped moving around and calls Palos Verdes Estates home. Seated in her exotically beautiful new house, Susie describes her youth in a military family as "the most positive experience" she ever had. "It taught me how to observe and adapt," a concept that she uses in life and work, along with "sensitivity and practicality."

"It was," she explains thoughtfully, "an adventure, but there were difficult times as well." She went to Coronado High School in the sixties during the Vietnam War with other military kids. Her father was on the aircraft carrier Ticonderoga. Susie has a particularly vivid memory of the family friend who taught her how to water-ski being shot down on her birthday. Several other friends became prisoners of war. "In the military," Susie explains, "one has to prepare for tragedy, so that's why you learn to enjoy life while you can."

She had fun, such as attending the Midshipman's Ball and other "carefree things." Susie also ran the babysitting desk at the Coronado Hotel and had a curfew. "It was great training," Susie says. "The attitude that we learned was a great love and respect of family; no one or nothing else mattered. The military taught us that and I live it today."

Close to her family and Ed's and her four adult sons, Susie enjoys family gatherings as well as charity parties. She opens her home to organizations like the Palos Verdes Art Center for whom she serves as member of the board. She and Ed also head up the Art Patrons group. She enjoys people feeling at ease in her home, a concept which she applies in her design work.

"I try to make people feel comfortable in their residence. When I create a design, I try to make it look like no designer has been there." Clients will often hand Susie the key and "not come back until I'm finished."

Susie's upbringing enables her, when she sees a new client, "to observe quickly and tune in to their desires." She sees "common sense and logic" as her strength in design, as well as understanding "scale and its relationship to the design." Her humor is applied in the "touches of whimsy" that she includes in all the homes she designs.

She and Ed travel often and both love to collect objects from places they've visited. Susie "loves unusual antique dishes and serving platters, even if I never use them." Before her move into her new home, she also collected jewelry. When she put all of it into a carry bag, it was so heavy she couldn't pick it up. "I weighed it and had 65 pounds of jewelry, so I decided that it was time to stop collecting," she laughs.

Susie enjoys cooking, "loves to read," and has a large collection of cookbooks suitable for their many theme parties. Life is still an adventure, and she still enjoys the travel, but now she intends to enjoy her new home. She looks forward most of all to the birth of their first grandchild in October. She will, of course, remain involved in her work and her art.

"Life is sometimes a fluke," Susie says. "I never thought I'd be where I am today. My father, who died two years ago, told me that one is never able to have a definitive opinion, because you never have all the facts. A situation is always the catalyst for something else."

It seems that the synergy of art and the military has been the catalyst to define this creative woman.

Palos Verdes Style Magazine (1995-1999)

Buddy Ebsen: From Beverly Hills Hillbilly to Palos Verdes Artist

PV Style, September/October 1995

When the Palos Verdes Beach and Athletic Club held its summer art exhibit, Buddy Ebsen was the featured celebrity artist and special guest. His beautiful wife Dorothy greeted visitors and proudly pointed out his serigraph "Sea Power," which depicts the Palos Verdes coastline.

Buddy first visited the Peninsula in 1935 and was ready to buy property, but studio advisers talked him out of it by reminding him that "it would take too long to get to the set." He always remembered the beauty of Palos Verdes, however, and has now been a resident for eight years. He began drawing sketches of the characters from his hit television series *Beverly Hillbillies* shortly after his arrival. Dorothy, herself a talented artist, recognized his artistry, and encouraged him to try his hand at painting. He, in fact, completed two classes at the Palos Verdes Art Center.

Dorothy is the most important of many ties to the area. They met at the Long Beach Yacht Club during the Congressional Cup Race and were married in Hawaii. After their marriage, they lived in a seaside condominium in Long Beach. A WWII Navy officer, Buddy's love of the sea and ships led him to design and oversee the building of his catamaran *Polynesian Concept* docked in San Pedro.

It was built to win the 1968 two-week San Pedro to Honolulu race, and it did! *The Swift of Ipswich,* which he considered buying as early as 1947, has been the subject of one of Buddy's paintings and is docked in San Pedro. It is now a training vessel for inner-city kids.

Many may not know that Buddy began his showbiz career as a dancer with the Ziegfield Follies. Six foot, three inches tall, with a handsome, expressive face and big grin, he was a megastar, both as a duo with his sister Velma, and as a single on the night club circuit. He danced with the likes of Ruby Keeler and Eleanor Powell.

What seems like a long way from his days as his favorite character Jed Clampett to painter is a natural evolution for Buddy. After all, this multi-talented man not only danced with both Shirley Temple and Judy Garland but taught them the dance numbers featured in their respective movies.

From musical star, he moved on to dramatic film roles such as *Breakfast at Tiffanys* with Audrey Hepburn. He then went to television where he starred in long running hits *Davey Crockett, Beverly Hillbillies, and Barnaby Jones*. And now he continues to use his talents in many areas.

Interviewed in his beautiful Palos Verdes home, Buddy describes the act of painting as "an incredible miracle." He is moved by color, "perhaps," he says, since his "life has been colorful."

He also enjoys the experience of creating something "that wasn't there before that people found pleasant to look at." When asked what it is about a completed work of his that defines a successful painting, he said it must, "most of all have totality of impact," visually and emotionally. Collectors agree and have snapped up his works at San Pedro and Beverly Hills galleries.

The quixotic moments of fate are not lost on him. He had to give up his role as the Tin Man in the classic *Wizard of Oz* when he became seriously ill from the aluminum powder the makeup people used. Although he underplays the seriousness of the situation, he was, in fact, near death from inhaling the toxic substance.

Buddy is philosophical, however, about life's crossroads, for each time something didn't work out, he chose another path and met with great success and long running hits. He describes himself as an optimist, a positive thinker who "circles and outflanks," searching for "the next possibility."

An avid reader, history buff, and writer, his story-filled autobiography *The Other Side of Oz* is another accomplishment of which he is most proud. He's currently working on a novel and writes plays, poems, songs, and has written a musical about Aimee Semple McPherson.

He, of course, loves traveling with wife Dorothy to places like Branson, Missouri, where he recently fulfilled another ambition, a one man show. In the meantime, this charming, talented man will continue with his painting, a talent that he can share with all of us that live on *this* side of Oz.

Eddy Hartenstein: President of DirecTV
PV Style Sept./Oct. 1996

DIRECTV, according to the literature, "offers one of the broadest arrays of programming selections available to consumers today." Received at consumers' homes by a DSS satellite receiving system which includes an 18-inch satellite dish, digital receiver, and remote control, the sophisticated but simple to operate equipment allows the consumer to scan an interactive on-screen program guide, and select programming via the remote control, including pay-per-view movies. If desired, the individual can also restrict access to selected channels, program favorite channels, and establish spending limits for movies. 175 direct channels, including all major cable TV networks and special interest programs, now reach 1.8 million households via broadcast satellite service with a goal to reach 10 million by the year 2000.

They say the true measure of a man can be observed in his personal relationships. Arriving at his El Segundo office, Rolling Hills resident Eddy Hartenstein, President of DIRECTV, found an injured employee being taken by gurney to a waiting ambulance. Following the individual to the street, he said some encouraging words while she was being put inside. His concerned demeanor was that of a family member. The concepts of family and team are, in fact, his watchwords.

Although Eddy—described by his co-workers as "brilliant"—is the dynamic force responsible for the overall development and operation of DIRECTV, a unit of Hughes Electronics Corporation. Since its inception in 1990, he credits the combined efforts of his management team for its success. Under his leadership, the company has become the "fastest growing entertainment distribution company in the world" in less than two years. Hughes Electronics recognized Eddy's personal achievements by recently appointing him a Corporate Vice President.

Eddy's father, a musician turned restauranteur, was born near Zurich, Switzerland. Eddy, a Los Angeles native, points out that his name being Swiss is not a derivation of Edward. The combination of a Swiss and American heritage may in fact explain something about his character.

He describes himself as a "cross between a perfectionist and a pragmatist who would like it right 100 % of the time, but the real world doesn't allow that. So, one has to get it right the first time. The risk of inaction becomes the higher risk, therefore, one has to grasp the opportunity, make the decision, delegate, and let someone else take over."

Eddy worked in the family-owned business, the Switzerland Restaurant. His understanding of how business affects the consumer on a personal level was developed there, as well as his love of cooking and good cuisine. Although his free time is limited, he enjoys cooking for his wife Cathy and two sons, Carl, eleven, and Christian, eight.

An outstanding student, he joined Hughes after receiving his BS degrees in Aerospace Engineering and Mathematics from California State Polytechnic university, Pomona, in 1971 and 1972 respectively. Eddy also received an MS degree in Applied Mechanics from Cal Tech in 1974 while a Hughes Aircraft Company Masters Fellow. Fluent in German and Swiss with a basic knowledge of Italian, French, and Spanish, he is proud to think of himself as a "self-made man coming from common roots." Being "capable and willing to do the most menial task alongside of you" marks the attitude of esprit de corps that Eddy encourages.

Recipient of many outstanding swards yet reluctant to speak of personal achievements and downplaying his intellectual prowess, Eddy describes his education as "great," an important tool necessary to achieve his aims. As a student, he had the "instincts and common sense to succeed." His experience in Hughes' various companies as well as NASA's Jet Propulsion Laboratory led to the skill of deal making; his entrepreneurial sense from talking and listening to people. He does acknowledge his ability for sorting and cataloguing details. "In order to understand the macro-level, one must appreciate things on a micro-level."

He finds life in Palos Verdes beautiful, quiet, and secure, and enjoys taking his boys to places like the nearby cliffs, Point Vicente Interpretive Center, and Ruby's. Although Cathy owns a horse and loves to ride, with his hectic schedule, Eddy seeks the more quiet and relaxing venues for what little free time he has. DIRECTV and four television sets in his home gives him the ability to select whatever his mood suggests. He especially loves music and has arranged for DIRECTV to be one of the benefactors of the October 13th Music Fair organized by the Peninsula Committee for the Los Angeles Philharmonic Orchestra. Reading works like Tom Wolfe, P.J. O'Rourke, and Garrison Keillor is another pastime.

Having no time for personal athletics, Eddy makes time for the boys' team sports. He works hard to meet his obligations to both his personal and Hughes families. He's very aware of his responsibility to the shareholders and works long hours, but he "tries to find a balance in the early morning hours, evenings and weekends. I want to be a great Dad and husband," he declares.

In philosophizing about personal attributable success, Eddy suggests that "no one person should delude themselves in thinking they're responsible for the success of DIRECTV." With many experts in the field of television, one can say, "with apologies to Descartes, I watch, therefore I am."

When asked how he would describe himself to someone who didn't know him or DIRECTV he said, "Normally one defines oneself as a job, but I think first of the fact that I have two boys and a wife—a great family—and I work for a great company called DIRECTV."

This too, it might be said, is another criterion for the true measure of the man.

Holiday Magic
PV Style, November/December 1995

It is fitting that the use of the term "magic" has come to be associated with the Christmas season. In the South Bay, there are many groups and individuals who work very hard to create magic with their wonderful illusions, and with much success. Over time, they have created traditions that have become an important part of the magical family holiday.

A Christmas Pageant

Among the oldest traditional events on the peninsula is the Christmas pageant at the Neighborhood Church of Palos Verdes. It is not certain whose idea it was to present living tabloids of the Christmas story, but it is believed to have started around 1953 during Dr. Richard Dawson's tenure as pastor.

Then as now, the pageant was organized as a series of scenes depicting the story of the first Christmas. Generally, the settings and locations on the church grounds were as they are today, including the use of live animals. The cast has continued to include church members and friends interested in participating.

In the early days, the costumes were simple bathrobes and whatever was available, including the old velvet drapes that once hung in the Haggerty house before it became the church. Angel wings were painted on cardboard. The costumes improved as current director Maxine Dessau used her creative talent and the talents of friends in Hollywood, where she worked many years, and congregation members who helped to sew the new designs.

The pageant continued to improve and grow as the group gained experience and new members. The Herod Scene acquired a new director when Robert Wright, producer of the Carol Burnett Show, volunteered along with members of the high school youth group. Although today there is a new director of the scene, the costume designs still demand youthful figures, so cast members continue to be high school students.

This year, due to the addition of the new Fellowship Hall, the production will involve some changes. Three of the scenes, The Annunciation, The Departure, and Shepherds in the Field, will be re-staged. As in productions past, the development of the program and its magical splendor will continue to add to the level of audience enjoyment.

The event will begin in the sanctuary where the story of the first Christmas will be read. The adult and children's choirs will then lead the audience in singing carols. From there, visitors will view the tableaux scenes on the grounds and return for refreshments and gift browsing.

Directors/Producers are Tricia Hopper and Sally Rogers. Barbara Selzer Johnson, wife of the current minister, is Costume Designer. Gene Ogle, Technical Director. Fran Brock, Music Director.

A Victorian Christmas

Another wonderful illusion that is beautifully recreated is the Victorian Christmas at the Banning Residence Museum. This will be the eighth year that the Nineteenth Century Greek Revival mansion, former home of General Phineas Banning, is presented in all its holiday splendor. There, visitors can step back in time and experience how a prosperous family lived and celebrated 100 years ago.

Banning was born in Wilmington, Delaware and arrived in San Pedro in 1851. He made his first fortune by creating a stagecoach line to the City of Los Angeles. He was a strong supporter of the Union during the Civil War and was appointed Brigadier General of the First Brigade of the State Militia.

At the end of the Civil War, he built his home, where visitors can experience the finest example of Greek Revival architecture in Southern California. Its eighteen rooms house an extensive collection of Victorian decorative arts, textiles, and furnishings from the period when it was the family residence.

Although a public facility, Friends of Banning Park raises the funds to make the ongoing restoration of the historic interiors and grounds possible. In addition to the house, the grounds include a Banning stagecoach barn, a one-room schoolhouse, and family gardens.

Open to the public all year, it is during the holiday season when it is most festive and a time "to renew [the] holiday spirit," says Director Zoe Bergquist. Visitors will be greeted by carolers in Victorian garb, bell ringers, and Santa in his Victorian carriage.

Since many guests come each year, the decor is never repeated. This year's theme is "Visions of Sugarplums." Christmas House Decorating Co-chairs Mary Jane Horn and Dee Edridge have some unique things planned.

Professional florists will use their special powers of illusion when lavish trees with period decorations, fresh greens, flowers, and hand-made ornaments grace each room. The dining room will be set for Christmas dinner, and the family living room and children's room will be filled with wonderful surprises. Banning Residence

Museum Volunteers, a group of about 120 active members, will act as room docents.

The museum shop will offer a Christmas collection of ornaments, toys, books, assorted gifts, homemade candy, breads, and cookies. It will be a time of enchantment when those that work their magic present a home filled with the sights, sounds, and smells of a Christmas 100 years past.

Admission includes a tour of the house, stagecoach barn and schoolhouse, demonstrations, entertainment and refreshments. The donation benefits museum educational programs.

A Christmas Drama Musical

Dr. David Halverson, Pastor of Worship, Music, and Creative Arts at Rolling Hills Covenant Church will use his inspirational creativity for the twelfth year when he brings together the talents of many individuals to create the church's annual Christmas Drama Musical. Chip Hipkins is Drama Director and Larry Pearsall is Technical Director.

There will be magical, extraordinary effects when the musical "From Heaven's Throne" is presented. An original written by David Clydesdale of Nashville, Tennessee, it is the Christmas story as experienced by the angels, and the entire story takes place in Heaven. The illusion of Heaven is created using thousands of tiny twinkling stars, angels in glittering robes, and other tricks of fantasy.

Debra Stipe, a member of Rolling Hills Covenant Church, will be the storyteller/soloist. In addition to performing the lead in many of the church's performances, Stipe has also appeared in several television productions. She played one season of the sitcom *Full House* and several episodes of *Murder, She Wrote* and *In the Heat of the Night*.

The Christmas season is a time for family and friends to come together and experience the meaning of the festive season. It is a time of joy and celebration filled with scenes of enchantment and wonder.

It is indeed a time that reflects the magic of love and the gift of giving. What better gifts of love are given than moments of magic brought to fruition through the talent and hard work of many individuals? Such are the gifts that are offered to the community during the magical Christmas holiday.

Artist Diane Bartz and Her Gift of Love
PV Style Nov./Dec. 1996

Internationally renowned Palos Verdes artist Diane Clapp Bartz expresses the spirit of Christmas year-round through the donation of her art, a true gift of love.

She is a philanthropic supporter of many charities such as the Spastic Children's Foundation and The Wellness Community which have benefited greatly from her generosity.

Her love of children has been recognized at the White House where she was received by First Lady Barbara Bush as an honored guest for her support of the International Craniofacial Foundation.

On Christmas Eve the most important gift is given to her family and extended family. Her parents lived in New Orleans when Diane was born, where they began a tradition of large Christmas Eve gatherings. It continued with their move to Texas and is carried on today by Diane.

"People who had nowhere to go at Christmas or had no family of their own were invited to my parent's home, along with friends and family, and now I open my home."

Diane estimates that the smallest group attending has been 30 people and the largest 67, always "with lots of kids."

Family and friends will arrive from Japan, Virginia, Texas, Florida, and various parts of California to celebrate this annual event. Diane has five adult children and eight grandchildren, so her immediate family stays overnight, "sleeping wherever there's room."

Diane explains that a typical Christmas Eve starts at Thanksgiving when names are drawn for the gift exchange.

"Everyone has to bring a gift and I make sure every child has one from Santa Claus." Albert Bartz, Diane's husband, has enjoyed playing this role for years.

When people arrive, they enjoy eggnog "so thick you can turn the glass upside down and it won't fall out."

A long time is spent catching up with family news, and then everyone joins hands and is led in prayer by Albert.

The serious business of eating then begins at tables set up throughout the house and studio. There may be no snow in Palos Verdes, but Diane's paintings of snowy scenes form an appropriate backdrop to the festivities.

Tradition reigns supreme. "When people come, they bring a potluck item," Diane says, "and if they don't make what they've made prior years, there's a riot!"

Diane's specialties include her version of Texas chili and Louisiana Creole squash. There are also Creole potatoes, chicken enchiladas, lasagna, and much more, including lots of desserts.

After dinner, Santa arrives with gifts for the children, after which the adults exchange theirs. Even the family dogs get presents and since the gifts are opened one at a time, it can go on for quite a while.

"There's always a lot of noise and excitement and it's great fun all evening. It's always hectic and a lot of work, but we love it so much-it's a gift of love I give to my family each year," Diane says.

Titanic's Historians
Don Lynch and Ken Marschall
PV Style, May/June 1997

The excitement was apparent as passengers boarded the great super liner for its maiden voyage on April 10, 1912. The ship was larger, more luxurious, and comfortable than other ships making the Atlantic crossing from England to New York.

A total of 1,324 passengers and a crew of 899 was aboard. The voyage ended abruptly four days later in a tragic event that took the lives of 830 passengers and 685 crew members.

On April 14 at 11:40 p.m., the great ship that was considered rival to none hit an iceberg. At 2:20 a.m. on the morning of Monday, April 15, it broke in two and tore apart. While those who had found safety in tiny lifeboats watched in horror, the magnificent ship plunged below the surface.

First the bow, then the stern disappeared into the dark, frigid waters, taking those unfortunates left behind. The great ship's name was Titanic.

The history of the tragedy and the events leading up to it are re-enacted in the mega-million-dollar film *Titanic*. Directed by James Cameron—noted for action thrillers—it will open in major theaters on July 2. Overseeing the accurate portrayal of the many heroic and tragic stories within the story and the accuracy of the ship's features was the job of technical advisers Don Lynch and Ken Marschall of Redondo Beach.

Author and illustrator respectively of *Titanic, An Illustrated History*, they capture most vividly every detail of the magnificent ship and its historic passengers.

Considered experts in the subject, they continue to preserve the experiences and stories of those aboard.

Using photographs of people and events on the Titanic, Director Cameron re-enacts them in the film. One photo, which is central to the storyline, depicts first class passenger Frederic Speddon watching his son play with a top. Don plays the role that, although a minor part, "was certainly a high point for me. Being in costume on the Titanic, even though it was a set, felt as if it was 1912."

A board member of The Titanic Historical Society, Don was an organizer of the Society's recent convention held on the Queen Mary in Long Beach. Present were two of the seven remaining survivors who were aboard ship. Both Don and Ken describe their friendships with survivors as "the greatest reward."

"It's ironic," Ken says, "that a ship that brought so much heartache can bring so much joy to our lives."

Owner of Matte Effects, Ken has done artwork for the movies *Winds of War, The Terminator,* and others. He has created over one hundred paintings of the Titanic for books, movies, and models—his first completed while in high school. To ensure its accuracy, he studied the ship's blueprints and photos from archives.

"I am a perfectionist, so the desire to know every nook and cranny has led to the wealth of knowledge I have about the ship."

He considers Don a "world expert," who also began his research at an early age. While in high school, he joined the Titanic Historical Society and was disappointed to find no survivors were members. Using passenger and other lists, he located them and their families. He did so well in his research that at the age of nineteen, he was invited by the Society to join the advisory board.

Don's friendship with survivors is "very special." At her death, Ruth Becker Blanchard of Santa Barbara left Don her scrapbook of memorabilia. In 1984, he planned the one hundredth birthday party for Edwina Troutt Mackenzie of Hermosa Beach, who died shortly after.

Being advisors on the film has been very exciting for both. Don observed that director Cameron "pays attention to historical and technical accuracy more than most would have."

Ken and Don agree that although the discovery of the wreck in 1986 was exciting, its poor condition was disappointing. Experts believed that the deep, cold water would preserve the ship intact. Ken also believes that salvagers have a "moral responsibility to return items to family members and not exhibit them."

Since this is the 85th anniversary of the tragedy, Ken and Don receive questions from around the world. Both agree it can get hectic, but at the same time, the public's interest keeps "the memory of the tragedy out there and honors those lost."

They believe the film will tell an accurate story of the events. "Special effects have reached the point technically where the sinking will be re-created in a very historical, realistic fashion. People will see for themselves what a beautiful ship it was and what a terrible ending it suffered."

International Chef Makes a Splash in Redondo Beach

PV Style, May/June 1997

An exciting, international star has arrived and he's making culinary waves at the new South Bay restaurant, Splash. He is world-renowned chef Serge Burckel, who is creating a level of expectation and generating an outpouring of superlatives normally reserved for rock stars. He is young, charming, good-looking, and talented, attributes which will cause restaurant-goers to sit up and take notice.

Adjacent to the Crowne Plaza Redondo Beach & Marina Hotel in Redondo Beach, California, Splash features a comfortable atmosphere and outstanding food. The facade features a fiber optic cable with undulating, waves of color. It welcomes patrons and sets the stage for what diners will encounter. Reflecting his experience in the glittering food capitals of the world, Chef Burckel's innovative cuisine is called Euro-Cal-Asian.

The epicurean fare he has developed is noted for its uniqueness and lightness. He moves away from traditional heavy sauces with emphasis on lighter blends such as his Linguini with Clams in a Light Seafood Stock, and the Roasted Rack of Lamb with mushrooms, tomatoes, and zucchini cake in a Pesto broth.

Chef Burckel selects the freshest of foods daily and combines unusual ingredients like the Turkey Confit Salad with Potatoes and Beets. The Asparagus Risotto with Grilled Sea Scallops is an example of how his artistic presentations please the eye as well as the palette.

Chef Burckel is a charming thirty-six-year-old man with a great smile, curly hair, and boyish qualities. When he begins to discuss his craft, he exhibits the intensity of an artist or athlete. These balanced qualities personify his individuality of personality and philosophy of food.

He has impressed often-unimpressionable food critics around the world. Using terms such as "a rare pearl," "a chef beyond compare," international food writers describe his approach in the kitchen as "inspirational," and "pure Heaven." Although Chef Serge's cuisine is referred to in these sophisticated terms, it is the creative simplicity of balance that is appealing.

He found his signature style through a systematic odyssey of experiencing the world's cuisines. Born in the Alsace region of France, Chef Burckel began a two-year apprenticeship at the age of sixteen, learning classical Alsation cuisine. After a required one-year tour of duty in the French military, he worked in one highly rated restaurant after another to learn his craft from the great chefs.

Among the settings was the Michelin five-star Hotel Des Trois Rois in Basel, Switzerland and its Rotisserie Des Rois; the Chantecler in the five star Hotel Negresco, Nice, where he worked with chef Jacques Maximin; and the only three star restaurant in Germany, Munich's Aubergine, with renowned chef Eckart Witzigmann.

In 1993, he made a move to the restaurant Belvedere at the Grand Stanford Harbor View Hotel in Hong Kong, where the restaurant was rated one of the four best dining rooms in the city. A Goose Liver Terrine was described by one reviewer as "not heavy in spite of the ingredients leading one to think that it should be rich."

Chef Burckel explains, "I respect the basic foundations taught to me...but I apply my original concepts. I do not believe in just copying recipes." At

Splash, the kitchen will be visible through a glass wall so diners will be able to watch him prepare his creations.

"Here in California, creativity and experimentation is more open," Serge says. "I intend to give good value for the money and look forward to welcoming clients in our beautiful setting." The South Bay certainly looks forward to seeing him.

Splash, opposite the beach, features a 6000 square foot interior bathed in a California color palette of eggplant, purple, pale gold, and teal. The room, which seats 102 patrons, commands a cozy and comfortable feeling.

It features a 350-gallon aquarium off the lounge area. A separate cigar bar enables the aficionado to experience a wide range of cigars in an intimate setting around a cozy fireplace. Separate patio seating is also available for cigar smokers and non-smokers.

Splash, located at 350 North Harbor Drive, Redondo Beach, adjacent to Crowne Plaza Redondo Beach Marina & Hotel, is open for dinner from 5:30 p.m. to 10:00 p.m. during the week and until 11:00 P.M on Friday and Saturday. Lunch service available soon.

The Empty Saddle Club
July/August 1997

On the edge of the northern corner of the Palos Verdes Peninsula in the middle of a residential area, is something quite unique: cattle. They share a colorful setting in Rolling Hills Estates with a resident Shetland Collie named Egypt who greets visitor at the entrance to the ranch. Roosters crow in the background. Dust swirls around the visitor's feet and a variety of exotic smells permeate the nostrils. Hay bales and horse trailers are everywhere and of course—horses. With names like Runt, Webster, Harlow, and Fleck, they occupy "barns" spread along the periphery of the property. The cattle are penned in corrals behind them. The twelve-and-a-half-acre spread is The Empty Saddle Club whose members are "active, western horsemen," and which existed before the incorporation of the city.

This may look, smell, and sound like a working ranch but, as club President John Sabio explains, "we are a riding club which offers a unique cattle use program in team roping, team penning, and cutting. The cattle we have at any one time vary according to the activities. Right now, we own twenty-three and rent another thirty. The cattle, bred for roping, are overseen by a veterinarian and are well cared for."

As eighty-six-year-old member and former business owner George Bradbury explains, the club "is a place to hone skills; to train horses, and to train the riders." His fifty-year membership may establish him as the club's senior member, but he is still quite active. He currently owns three quarter horses and has been in "racing, rodeo, ranching."

Ranching historically dominated the peninsula. The Dominguez family began to graze their herds in 1784 on land that extended from the San Pedro harbor to the Palos Verdes Peninsula. They were followed in 1821 by the Sepulvedas. Sixteen thousand acres of Rancho Los Palos Verdes was partitioned to cattle rancher Jotham Bixby in 1887. Harry Phillips, range manager for the Bixbys, also began his own ranch and in 1894 built his house near what is now the Rolling Hills gate at Palos Verdes Drive North. His subsequent ranch was on land near the present location of the Empty Saddle Club.

According to member William D. Canfield's history of the club, it was started in 1935 by "five horsemen from Redondo Beach and the surrounding area…who organized to participate in parades and other civic functions," as well playing broom polo. The story goes that a horse slipped and fell during a parade, losing its rider. A jesting remark was made about the empty saddle and the name of the group was born.

A permanent home was established with the purchase of the current site for $2900 on April 24, 1941. It was bordered by "the Chandler Ranch on the South and the Weston Ranch on the North." The roping arena, completed that autumn, is about the same today as it was then. An Army barracks acquired in 1947 remained the original clubhouse until it was replaced in 1995.

Although ranching is a thing of the past on the peninsula, the healthy outdoor lifestyle is not. Eighty-four active club members participate in trail rides, the training the cattle program, roping competitions, cookouts, horse shows, and rodeos. "Here, it's practice, practice, practice," John explains. "We have jackpot incentives, but we primarily train and work horses."

An up-and-coming roper is sixteen-year-old Brett Berry, son of member Roger Berry, who recently won two saddles, a horse trailer, and a thousand dollars. Another outstanding horseman who learned to rope at the club is nineteen-year-old college student Dugan Kelly, son of member Dr. Larry Kelly. He holds the 1996 High School National Championship Team Roping title.

Women have always enjoyed club privileges and participated in events, achieving a level of competence like roper Carol Ludwig. The first to attain full membership, however, was attorney Barbara Franzreb. She was admitted in September 1993 after the death of her member father.

Other Western and English riding groups use the facilities, including the Palos Verdes Peninsula Horsemen Association, Equestrian Trails Inc., and the Happy Hoofers, a women's horse and rider drill team. The city of Rolling Hills Estates also holds their yearly City Celebration on the grounds.

A recent historic event occurred with the first recorded calf birth on March 8, 1997. Originally named Norman but changed to Norma Jean after the vet's examination, she now lives on a Temecula ranch with her new owner, member Dick Pierce.

Since John, with George's advice, helped in getting the mother to feed the calf, the bovine baby seemed to think John was also a relative.

"I got that straightened out fast," he explains. "This club is quite a place! I'm not going to join a rodeo—but I sure have a great time here!"

It appears that everyone does—including the four-legged residents.

Jazz Pianist David Benoit from Bop to Ballet
PV Style September/October 1997

If creativity is a result of genes or environment, Palos Verdes resident David Benoit has all his ivories covered. As a boy, he literally slept with his piano. It shared the bedroom of his Bakersfield home. His mother Betty played piano and his father Bob, a college professor, played jazz guitar on weekends. It seemed a certainty that he would end up in music.

However, he also loved architecture, building, and interior design. He studied everything he could on the subjects and believed that's what he wanted to do in life. His criteria for "a great house," he says laughingly, "was one with a sub-zero refrigerator!" Fortunately for his fans, music won out and "consumed everything."

"I always had a feel for the piano... [As a boy] I wanted to make music without doing the work." David's mother tried to teach him the piano, but "it just didn't come together." Although he couldn't read or write music, he taught himself to play by ear. He wrote "little songs," recording them on an old Wollensak recorder.

In the early 60's, the family moved to Hermosa Beach, but the piano didn't move with them. They were without one for four years and David really missed it. By that time, he was fourteen and "lived and breathed music." After they bought another piano, the formal training began, and by the age of sixteen David knew he wanted to be a "famous jazz performer."

After high school, he went to El Camino College and studied Theory and Composition. However, he was eager to go to Hollywood because it was "filled with musicians." He spent ten years there doing studio work, accompanying vocalists, and playing weddings and parties.

He made a recording on a small label that wasn't well-known here. It was, however, very big in the Philippines and became a hit record. In 1981, David was invited to do a concert there and says, "it was a total surprise; a shock." The venue turned out to be the 3,000 seat Philippine Cultural Center with a 21-piece orchestra and his name in lights ten-feet high.

"I went from playing bar-mitzvahs to superstar overnight. I thought to myself, from now on, it's all going to be like this." But it wasn't. Back in the States, David had agreed to play at a wedding. "When I showed up at the front door carrying my electric piano, they sent me to the back to stay in the kitchen with the cooks. I never played those settings again."

He had gained enough confidence in the Philippines to leave his studio career and "focus on being a solo jazz artist" and his composing. He spent 1982 and 1983 honing his skills at the Manhattan Bar and Grill in the South Bay, where he acquired a large following. His fans, who enjoyed his "trademark melodic sound," showed up to support him at his first appearances at the Greek Theater.

David's musical life reflects his diversity and talent. "My personality is such," he says, "that I always want things to be exciting and interesting." His list of accomplishments—performer, composer, arranger, film scorer, conductor for stage, film, and television—shows the breadth and depth of his versatility.

He has developed his craft over the years as he worked with a myriad of talent such as Miles Davis, Eric Marienthal, David Pack, and at a recent Hollywood Bowl performance, Dave Brubeck. He has appeared with the

Los Angeles Philharmonic, the San Francisco Symphony, and others. His work is described as "truly the best of contemporary jazz."

David describes his transition on his new album *American Landscape* with the London Symphony Orchestra as "a fusion of symphonic music and popular music." This work "reflects his growth," and shows his "new areas of interest." It includes a tribute to his mother, who passed away this year.

His movement into the classical mode includes his "symphonic composition" *Kobe,* which tells the story of a Japanese girl growing up in Japan after the bombing of Hiroshima. The story, partly inspired by another family member—his mother-in-law, who lives near Kobe—will later be choreographed as a ballet.

This Grammy nominee will demonstrate his jazz style by "returning a favor to a community that has been good to me." David will appear with several jazz friends and surprise guests at the Peninsula Music Fair on October 5 on the grounds of Chadwick School.

His ties to the South Bay are solid. He was able to fulfill his love of architecture and building through participating in the design of his Torrance recording studio. That pleasure will be further enhanced when he and wife Kei build their dream house on the peninsula.

One can be sure that it will have a piano, a sub-zero refrigerator, and of course—music.

A Reflection of Light and Color
Palos Verdes Style, November/December 1997

"We lived in this house about five years before we remodeled the kitchen," explains Gail Temianka. She and her physician husband Daniel, who is Medical Director of Health Care Partners Medical Group, knew when they purchased their Palos Verdes Estates residence that it was a must.

The original kitchen was a dark, open space, and although it was large, did not have the charm and conveniences that Gail wanted. Since it was the last room in the house to be redone, she knew exactly what she wanted, and wished to be involved in the design process. That's where Peveler's Custom Interiors entered the picture.

Working with Sue Van Every, Gail articulated her needs and design ideas. An important requirement was that the work be completed in time for her daughter's school orchestra fundraiser she was hosting at her home. The goal was met, and the 415 square foot kitchen took nine weeks from concept to completion.

The color scheme was planned around the hand-selected almond mauve granite countertop with an Ogee bull-nose edge. Flecked with multi-colors, it picks up the turquoise color of the pool seen from the re-designed sink window.

A three-piece glazed, ceramic tile bas-relief panel behind the Thermador professional cooktop features a textured fruit and lattice design. Custom colored, it establishes the accent color palette of turquoise, pink, mauve.

Finished with four-inch turquoise tiles, the wall becomes an important focal point and establishes the English Country look Gail wanted.

The raised panel cabinets are painted a custom color of creamy white. It was the "most difficult selection, requiring about fifteen visits to the paint store for samples." Inspired by the fabric used for the window treatment, the color creates the "airy, light finish" Gail wanted.

A double-detailed chair-rail placed at plate-rack height tops a composition bead-board paneling used throughout that works to tie the room together. The use of a wide crown moulding at the ceiling finishes off the coordinated look.

Three main areas of the room create separate focal points: the cooking area, sitting area, and eating area. A center island divides the space yet creates multi-use sections.

An overstuffed floral sofa in the sitting area faces a built-in television. Above is a cabinet filled with pink depression glass. Lining either side are bookshelves with stained glass doors. Stained glass panels from the Temianka's former residence were redesigned to pull the color scheme together in a charming scene of branches, birds, and butterflies. It is topped with a custom-designed arched valence with cut-outs of cherries taken from the tile panel design. This is mirrored in the opposite side of the room in the plate-rack cabinetry next to the sink window.

The preparation side of the island has a mixer lift which brings the appliance to counter height. A spice drawer with angled shelf allows easy viewing and selection. Trays and platters are stored below in custom sized compartments. The busy cook can chat with family or friends seated at bar stools at the dining end of the island.

Opposite is a stainless-steel double sink that overlooks the pool and garden. This section has the dishwasher and compactor and additional storage space. Adjacent is Daniel's special built-in, a "coffee garage" with a roll top. It holds the coffeemaker on a roll-out shelf.

The arched valence cabinet on the further side of the window has a recessed shelf especially created to hold a ceramic rabbit Gail painted.

Everything is located only a few steps away. The dining table and china hutch are convenient to the island and sits in a bright, cheery area close to the sliding door to the deck and pool below. Next to the eating area is a built-in roll-top desk with file drawers. Above is a cabinet with glass pane doors containing more pink depression glass. Overhead recessed lighting provides a well-lit work area.

Immediately to the right is a walk-in pantry with a pocket door. Thirty-eight square feet, it is Gail's pride and joy. Lined with adjustable shelves, it provides plenty of storage. Built-in wine racks and linen drawers add a special touch.

The cooking area has Thermador appliances throughout and features the professional cooktop with grill, a warming drawer, convection oven, two microwave ovens, including a convection microwave, and the 48-inch refrigerator with matching raised-panel doors.

Additional storage is also provided. The range hood cabinet constructed on the job uses a special design that allows the display of a large decorative platter.

The room is further enhanced with a creamy color composition floating floor. With the look of hand-painted planks, it is decorated with flowers picking up the selected color scheme. The ceiling height remained the same, but recessed lighting was added throughout to provide the cozy, yet necessary practical lighting.

The function and charm of the room appear to be an extension of Gail's personality and lifestyle. The decor is ever changing depending upon the season. Using her extensive collection of House of Hatten figures, antique glass, and her own crafts and hand-painted ceramics, Gail adds to the warmth and color of her beautiful kitchen.

"We found just what we wanted in the Peveler group," Gail explains. "Ron Peveler, Sue, Douglas, and the crew were great. We trusted them so much we went off on vacation while they were here. They were outstanding. The design and flow work, and the room is light and inviting. I got just what I asked for."

Reinhold Ullrich M.D.:
Mountain Climbing Physician
PV Style, January/February 1998

He looks like the average American man. He is unassuming and rather reluctant to tell his story. When asked what acquaintances would say if he shared his experiences, he responded, "They wouldn't believe me. I don't usually talk about it, so they'll be surprised," to hear that Reinhold Ullrich, obstetrician-gynecologist of forty years, is a mountaineer, outdoor adventurer, and sportsman.

Rolling Hills resident since 1959 and father of six, Dr. Ullrich's dream was to climb and reach the summit of the highest mountain on each of the seven continents. He made it to the top of six and was with an expedition on Mount Everest in 1995, but "did not reach the peak."

Sitting in his home surrounded by a lifetime of exotic memorabilia from around the world, the former President of the Los Angeles County Medical Association relived his days on the mountain.

"A hazardous area among many on Everest is the ice fall. It is like a river rapid that has become frozen and has many crevices."

Located near the beginning of the climb, "we go up it and back at least six times to practice, and also to climatize ourselves before the actual ascent. We did it successfully on the practices. On the climb itself, I slipped on the ice falling into a small crevice, and fractured and dislocated my elbow." Disappointed and with a splintered arm, he waited at base camp while the expedition continued the climb. Although the most sophisticated and high-tech gear is used on Everest and they were well-prepared, "the weather is the most risky and changeable...things can suddenly happen." The weather turned bad and after five days, the group returned to base, canceling the remainder of the trip.

Dr. Ullrich was raised in Pittsfield Massachusetts in the middle of the Berkshires. As a boy, he "liked the challenge of unusual things" and spent time climbing the scenic mountains.

In 1944, at the age of seventeen, he enlisted in the Army. He spent one and a half years at the end of World War II at the Panama Canal, where he hiked. When he returned home "eager to catch up with life," he attended Berkshire Business College, later applying to Harvard University where he graduated in an accelerated program in Biochemical Science. ·- .

He finished medical school at State University of New York at Buffalo in 1953 and immediately married Nora Boland, a nurse he met at one of the hospitals. Two days later, they drove to California where he spent his internship and residency at Harbor General Hospital. Since he began his practice in 1957, he has been affiliated with Torrance Memorial Hospital and Little Company of Mary Hospital.

At the age of forty, he began to run in marathons, doing three to four per year. He's participated in Berlin, London, Montreal, Seoul, has run in Boston twelve times, and even ran in a marathon above the Arctic Circle. Usually completing in under four hours, he came in first in his age group in St. George, Utah, "which was quite exciting. Running is also the best preparation for climbing."

Dr. Ullrich's interest in serious climbing first developed at Mammoth Mountain, where the family went skiing. He later took a basic rock-climbing course in the Grand Tetons. The level of difficulty increased when he took a trip to Mexico in 1959 with the Sierra Club and climbed three ice and snow-covered volcano peaks.

The challenge was heightened when he decided it would be interesting to climb the highest mountains in North America, South America, Europe, and Antarctica, which he did. Then came the attempt "to try for the seven continents," he says matter of factly.

"Of course," Dr. Ullrich explains, "all of this took time." The first big one he attempted and completed was Mt. McKinley in Alaska.

"It took three tries before I made the peak of one of the most difficult, Irina Jaya in Indonesia."

Known among followers of the sport, he has been team physician on several climbs. He has many friends among the mountain climbers and, sadly, knew several who perished in their attempts.

He is reticent about sharing anecdotes, so his wife Nora told the story of his "heroic act" on a mountain peak in South America. A Japanese climber was missing, and Dr. Ullrich went to the top, where he found him. Since it was too dark to descend, he waited until morning, when he brought him down, "saving his life."

Dr. Ullrich has parachuted, earned his pilot's license, river-rafted, run the 100-mile Western States Endurance Run, been on an African safari, and trekked the North pole.

"It is most exciting to reach the summit and get back home safely to Palos Verdes, the most beautiful part of the world."

He should know. He has seen most of it—from the top.

Lowell H. Greenberg, M.D., Photographer of Nature's Exotica

PV Style March/April 1998

To relieve the stress of his professional life, he visits exotic cultures, swims with the sharks, runs with the bulls in Pamplona, and photographs it all. He is Medical Oncologist Lowell H. Greenberg of the Cancer Care Associates.

A Palos Verdes Estates resident, Dr. Greenberg faces life and death crises daily in his practice. "I'm very involved with my patients and the strain is tremendous." Getting away to do the things he enjoys "cleanses the mind," and helps him "find a balance with life in oncology." Returning home "clear-headed and rejuvenated" allows him to continue his work of over 35 years at the demanding level it requires.

Born in Brooklyn, N.Y., he received his BS in 1953 at Tufts University and his MD from New York University in 1957. He came to Los Angeles for a residency in Medicine at the Veteran's Administration Hospital and was Clinical Associate in Hematology at UCLA Medical Center. He was a Fellow in Hematology at the New England Medical Center in Boston and not long after completion returned to California to start his practice.

One aspect of travel that gives Dr. Greenberg great pleasure is photography. His work lines the walls of his clinic, creating interesting and colorful vignettes of places he has visited. Portraits include lions, gorillas, an African mother and child, sunsets and beaches, and many others. Most unusual, however, are the underwater scenes.

Using an underwater camera, he enables the viewer to share a part of life under the sea in a way that the average person will never experience. Most tropical diving takes place in reefs. "You can't imagine what it's like," he explains. "They teem with life, and the colors and impressions vary depending on the type [of reef] and location."

Since the film in the camera can't be reloaded underwater, it's always a challenge to find the "best shots." His successes include many vivid examples such as the Butterfly, Lion, Clown, and Heniochus fish.

Always athletic and a member of the basketball team at Tufts, Dr. Greenberg took scuba diving lessons 25 years ago as a "family thing." Now that most of his eight children are grown and away from home, he and wife Margo continue the diving trips.

Certified by the Professional Association of Diving Instructors, Dr. Greenberg insists that diving "is not dangerous." The worst thing he experienced was "getting very seasick on a horrible thirty-six-hour trip in rough water in open ocean." They were with a group of divers heading to Cocos Island, the largest uninhabited island in the world. Located 300 miles off the coast of Costa Rica, it is the "best diving place in the world," and the "hub of deep-water fish."

Since no one is allowed on the island, they stayed on the boat for ten days to dive and photograph the hammer-head shark. Schools of 20,000 are found in the deep waters of the volcanic reef. "They don't eat you," he laughed, "because they're very shy. They think of you as another big fish and leave you alone."

Immersing himself totally in the experience, Dr. Greenberg subscribes to several diving magazines, and reads voraciously about potential destinations. He works hard to find the more remote and exotic visits such as

Papua, New Guinea, and trips down African rivers. But the diving trips particularly test his photographic skills.

A favorite one was to Two Brothers, uninhabited islands in the Red Sea that are reefs located five hours from the closest village on the Egyptian coast. There are shallow reefs and deep water with a "lot of life." Soft coral reefs are described as "shades of red and green bushes and stands [of coral], anemone, and colorful fish. Schools of red fish dart around in the blue background.

After a photo dive, the Greenbergs met with many large, aggressive sharks. Dr. Greenberg described how the sharks charged them and then veered off, "definitely not their normal behavior." Getting out of the water as quickly as they could, they climbed into the boat where the reason for the shark's "frenzy" became clear. The workers were "playing a game" in which they threw bait into the water to attract them. He later found out that they were Silky sharks—fifth on the list of the world's most dangerous. Maintaining that this was an unusual situation, Dr. Greenberg stresses that if equipment is properly cared for and one "follows the diving rules," everything is fine. The deepest he has gone is 160 feet and he's never happier than after the dive."

This Associate Clinical Professor of Medicine at U.C.L.A. Medical Center and Medical Director (Oncology) at Little Company of Mary Hospital is a highly skilled and successful Oncologist. The one thing he wants to be better at is outside of his profession— photography. He has plans to take a course in Photography—The National Geographic Way, and belongs to the Underwater Photographer Society, from which he has won awards for his photos. There is no doubt that he will achieve his goal on one of his next exotic trips.

The Whales of Randy Puckett Showcased in Palos Verdes

PV Style, March/April 1998

Suspended in a moment of the cycle of life, the great creatures are captured in bronze by their artistic creator. They are the whales of Randy Puckett.

The artist will be in Palos Verdes to present his work. The limited-edition bronzes will be displayed at an invitation only exhibit and reception on Friday, April 24 and Saturday, April 25, 1998, at a private residence.

The collection, which is shown for the first time in the area, has been sculpted by long-time whale admirer Puckett to show their magnificent, detailed beauty. His creations, which began in 1976 with a small wood carving for his son, have grown to life-sized versions that hang from the ceiling of the Hall of Marine Mammals in the Monterey Bay Aquarium.

Carving various animal forms since childhood, Southern Californian Puckett is an expert on whales and dolphins. Using photos, film, and scientific literature, he also researches each detail through unique personal observation such as post-mortem examination. In addition, he was permitted to dive with underwater biologists, during which he observed whale behavior.

His love for detail inspired him in 1981 to work in bronze. Not only does this medium give him more freedom of expression, but it enables Puckett to create the patina, or coloration, that is best suited for his indoor sculptures.

Combining abstract and realism, Puckett often develops the fluid form first, creating movement in space. From this starting point, he selects the theme of the conceived portrait. At other times, the activities of the whale will be the basis and foundation of the piece itself. All his sculptures tell a story and capture the grace and beauty of the ballet-like motions of these wonderful creatures.

"Newborn" is a splendid example. The mother is depicted gently lifting her baby up through the ocean levels, cradling it on her massive head. The feeling of movement is accentuated by the curling waves under her body. Another piece, "Twin Breach," portrays two Humpbacks clearing the water as they leap in unison through the waves. Forever held above the dancing swells, this piece personifies the wish of every whale watcher to see them rise out of the water in an acrobatic leap.

The graceful spiral of "Family" enables the viewer to observe the adult whales pass the skills necessary for survival to their offspring. Other pieces recreate dances of courtship, an expectant mother, and whales at play.

Randy Puckett has been involved with animals and the environment since he was a child. His love for the whales is reflected in his award-winning work. Displayed in galleries and museums throughout the world as well as private collections, he is recognized in both the art and scientific world.

The recipient in 1988 of the John Stoneman Marine Environment Award, he was acclaimed for his "outstanding contributions toward the better understanding and appreciation of the marine environment." In addition, the Scripps family commissioned Puckett to create a life-size sculpture of California Grey Whales entitled "The Legacy," which is displayed in the Scripps Institute in La Jolla.

Palos Verdes Art Center's
Executive Director Scott Ward
PV Style, May/June 1998

The world of Scott Ward is viewed within a philosophy of dualities. His position as Executive Director of the Palos Verdes Art Center combines his love of the arts and education. His work in photography expresses the "duality of life."

Scott describes his photographs as expressive of "right-brain, left-brain," a term that may aptly be applied to his life and career. Understanding his philosophy allows insights into his art and personality.

He is "more interested in the importance of the process of art rather than the object." That is, "art in its own making is therapy, a lifestyle, and [it] mediates the world. It can change our lives." His life changed when his wife Julie, serving on jury duty, learned through a fellow jurist and the mother of the former art center director, of the available position in Palos Verdes.

Scott and Julie, a practicing corporate litigator, currently make their home in Pasadena with their two children, ten-year-old Shannon, and nine-year-old Colin.

The youngest of three, Scott grew up in a military environment and describes his parents with pride. His father Bill, a career officer and Colonel at retirement was an architect who designed buildings for the Air Force. His mother Patricia, who passed away four years ago, had "inherent physical difficulties due to arthritis, but was strong and resilient and always kept going."

When Scott was three years old, the family was assigned to Morocco. His home is filled with artifacts from the region and strong feelings and memories of the three-year stay remain with him. After another three-year assignment in New Mexico, the family went to Lompoc, California, where Scott attended high school.

"Growing up there during the anti-war movement, I had a very strong sense of fairness and justice and the dignity of people. They are core values that stuck with me."

Probably also influenced by his earlier observations of other cultural groups, his "progressive ideas" and interest in social issue developed. Photography gave him a vehicle to express his philosophy and to "record bits of the world."

Scott credits his teachers with helping him to formulate thoughts and express himself. When he moved on to UC Santa Cruz, he found a "very exciting, creative setting" where he could experiment with art and ideas. He graduated with a B.A. in Aesthetic Studies with Honors for his Senior Thesis in 1977.

He attended graduate school at Cal Arts on a James Irvine Scholarship, where he was exposed to a system that recognized individual initiative. This developed in him the notion that "anything was possible."

Originally planning on a career in social service, Scott returned instead to his first love—photography. He received his M.F.A. in Photography in 1979.

"I believe photographs are visual sociology which enables the artist to make social statements." He finds interest in comparing and contrasting "public and private images." He does this through the use of diptych, combining two images to make a single photograph "more complex."

Scott spent years as an exhibiting artist and moved into curator and lecture work. His diverse experience runs the gamut from working artist to budget and business development. Head of the Downey Museum for ten years and a current lecturer at the university and college level, he is also partner in an eighty-thousand square foot performing arts center in San Francisco.

Downey Museum reflects his dual roles of artist-director in that he succeeded in broadening its artistic reputation and visual presence. He also enlarged the staff and met payroll, a business accomplishment of which he's most proud.

Having seen other arts organizations grow too quickly and not be sustainable, Scott's desire is that things be done in "incremental steps" at the art center. A strategic plan has been completed and includes, among other things, ways to make the art center more appealing to the public.

Surrounded by children, staff, and volunteers at a recent art center event, Scott is very gracious and outgoing with everyone. He's been busy increasing staff, meeting the "very important" volunteers, and interacting with the public. He wants to "outreach more to the community so that they know they are welcome here."

He's delighted that his work as an artist introduced him to the Palos Verdes community and he may one day exhibit his photography as another way for people to get to know him. His subjects are his children and "reflect the calm and somber aspect of kids."

They are happy memories that mirror his early views in a "mellowed dovetail of cultural beliefs relating to the dignity of people." His philosophy of duality diverges to create an artistic whole in the person of Scott Ward.

The Aquarium of the Pacific

PV Style, July/August 1998

Although we live on the edge of the Pacific Ocean, most of its inhabitants are unknown to us. Now the opportunity to become acquainted with its thousands of residents is available with the recent opening of the $117 million Aquarium of the Pacific in Long Beach.

Located on a five-acre site next to the Rainbow Harbor, the architecture of the 156,735 square foot aquarium mirrors the undulating waves of the nearby ocean.

Through the creation of three major exhibit galleries, the aquarium offers a look at more than 10,000 creatures and 550 different species that occupy the world's largest and most diverse body of water. The permanent exhibits feature life under the sea in the regions of Southern California and Baja, Northern California, and the Tropical Pacific.

A 5,200 square foot gallery is the setting for special exhibits. In addition, the aquarium's appeal for all ages is highlighted by the Kid's Cove play and learn area, "touch tanks" for adults and children, an auditorium, two classrooms, and a teacher's resource center.

In creating a self-contained learning experience, the aquarium provides individuals the services of a "comprehensive and technologically advanced" facility. A million gallons of Pacific saltwater fills the 17 major exhibit tanks and 30 smaller tanks used to house the marine life.

Once a month, new sea water is replaced in each living tank exhibit. The water is collected two to four miles offshore of Long Beach to ensure the most pollution-free collection. A filtering process takes place in the tanks every 30 to 90 minutes to maintain a clean and healthy environment.

Caretakers at the aquarium are aquarists, usually biologists, marine mammologists, and others. Not only are they responsible for the health and feeding of the marine life, but many will also be called upon to procure new specimens. Therefore, all are certified divers.

Designers of the facility have made sure that everyone's visit will be a pleasure. Upon entering, large dramatic tanks offer a taste of what lies in store. Suspended overhead is a full-scale model of the Earth's largest living creature—the blue whale. Nearby, the three stories high Predator tank contains sharks and barracuda.

The seal and sea lion exhibit offer an above and below water view. The mammals swim underwater through an acrylic tunnel. Visitors may then move to an outdoor arena where they can observe them sunning and playing above the water. Many of the animals have come to the aquarium from marine mammal rehabilitation centers and cannot be released into the wild.

Other popular exhibits include the sea otters, octopuses, and the largest exhibit—the 350,000-gallon habitat that includes a visual trip through the coral reefs to view the colorful corals and animal life.

Visitors can take a break in the indoor-outdoor restaurant overlooking the Queen Mary. A gift shop offers marine-themed gifts and souvenirs.

118

Summer Weekend Getaway:
La Quinta Resort & Club
PV Style, July/August 1998

In the 1930's, Hollywood great Frank Capra called La Quinta Resort & Club "a wonderful green oasis in the middle of the desert." The summer season is a great time to visit since this luxury retreat offers loads of activities and a restful retreat at a great value.

One can enjoy a romantic weekend, a golf package, or fun with the family. This beautiful setting provides it all. Spanish style one and two-story casitas with traditional adobe walls and red clay tiled roofs have views of the gardens and mountains. They provide a comfortable, cool home away from home.

Set against the Santa Rosa mountains, the beautiful grounds are filled with towering palm trees and beautiful flowers. Rather than one giant pool, there are twenty-five swimming pools and whirlpool spas scattered throughout the complex. Built in courtyard settings, many of the bungalow-type casitas face a pool, allowing easy and private access.

La Quinta's family package includes deluxe accommodations and free meals for children ages 5 to 12. Camp La Quinta provides supervised activities for the kids, allowing parents free time to use the fitness center, shop, or play tennis on one of thirty courts.

Known as one of the world's greatest golf resorts, the resort has two summer golf packages. With several courses to choose from, the golfer can select the one that meets the challenge and skill level desired. Each course is visually stunning with dramatic vistas.

For those who love to eat, two outstanding restaurants, Morgan's and Adobe Grill, provide a tasty experience for the whole family without having to leave the grounds. Morgan's is open daily for breakfast, lunch, and dinner, and Adobe Grill is open for dinner.

Morgan's offers an interesting choice of American cuisine, including the best Cobb Salad in the desert. The breakfast buffet includes hot and cold dishes. The lunch and dinner menu provides a wide selection. A poached, cold salmon plate is refreshing, and there is an interesting choice of pasta and meat dishes.

Adobe Grill is a fun experience in refined regional Mexican cuisine. The colorful setting offers dining in the restaurant or on the patio. Families can enjoy fresh guacamole prepared tableside, which is not to be missed, an unusual gazpacho served in an avocado, and mini quesadillas ranchera.

Entrees are varied and include a fantastic thinly sliced New York strip, served with a spicy black fire salsa. For fish lovers, the fresh halibut with a maple pecan crust and sweet Texas onion-orange butter sauce is delightful.

So, whatever your interests—golf, tennis, fine cuisine, or just kicking back and doing nothing—get away to this legendary oasis in the desert. It's a very special place.

John Koenig of Toyota Motor Sales
Races to the Future
PV Style, July/August 1998

When Rolling Hills Estates resident John Koenig was
growing up, like all young men, he wanted a car. Today
one can say he has the pick of the lot.

He has spent his adult life in the automotive industry
and has been with Toyota Motor Sales, U.S.A. since
1977. Currently he is Vice President of Motorsports at
Toyota Motor Sales, U.S.A., Inc. and president and chief
executive officer for Toyota Racing Development,
U.S.A., Inc.

He is involved in what most people view as a very
glamorous field—car racing. It's filled with unique,
competitive drivers guiding colorful, technological
marvels at incredible speeds. Extra excitement is
generated by the big earnings.

"This is our third season with Championship Auto
Racing Teams, which is the ultimate competition in
racing," John explains. Toyota provides the engines used
in the "champ" cars and John attends each event with a
technical team. He is on hand to "assist the teams,
monitor the engines, their installation and proper use,
and make necessary decisions."

"This season has gone reasonably well for us," he
reports. He has just returned from Portland, Oregon
where one of their drivers, Max Papis, had shown a
respectable finish. In John's office is an official racing
helmet signed by Papis. "Public relations and marketing
are my [other] reasons for being on hand." He meets with
the media to provide potential stories and set up
television interviews. In the local community, he serves

as chairman of the Board of Managers for the Torrance-South Bay YMCA.

Unlike the movies, a weekend of racing is not filled with parties and champagne. "I'm on my feet all day and do much walking, so I get plenty of exercise," John says laughing. "The race itself is lots of fun and very exciting."

John was born in New Baltimore, Maryland near Detroit. It was probably inevitable that he would be in the automobile field. "Growing up in the 50's and 60's, all guys were into cars. I had a paper route and saved my money so that I could buy one." His parents wouldn't allow it, but they gave him their old car. He fixed up the body and replaced the transmission, "something which I wouldn't do now. That was pretty tough."

John completed an engineering degree. College was a "struggle" because he was in a cooperative program in which he alternated semesters with work and school,

Upon graduation, John was employed by Ford motors as a body engineer. A stylist designed the model and John's job was to figure out how to make it work. He loved it, but quickly realized that the business development side of things would be most challenging. He attended Wayne State University in Detroit, completing the MBA program in 1974.

John had been unable to spend much time on hobbies. He did play ice hockey from the age of five years old until he was thirty and also played baseball. Since he had no money, he didn't take up skiing until he was 22 years old. Now, he and his wife Cindy and their children Colby and Callan ski every year at Mammoth.

He started with Toyota in 1977 and his responsibilities for Toyota Motor Sports activities include the company's Indy car, off-road racing, and Toyota Atlantic

Championship race programs. They're also sponsors of the Long Beach Grand Prix.

John has visited Japan 100 times during his career. Since he wears many hats in the company, there is little time on these trips for cultural activities. In his position with Toyota Racing Development, he also has responsibility for finance, business and technical development activities, and aftermarket sales.

Although John has never been in a race, he did attend racing school at Laguna Seco Raceway in Monterey, eventually driving at 110 m.p.h. "It was great fun. It helped me to understand what's involved in racing." This now qualifies him to take the second level and get a professional license. "I don't think there's much call for a beginning racer in his fifties," John chuckles.

He did do club motocross racing at one time and still has his bike. "In that sport, you have to fix everything that broke, so I'd race on a Wednesday, and it would take six days to repair everything. It was rather time-consuming."

Obviously, all his experiences helped in his profession. Knowing how things work and how to put it together led to great success. John was instrumental in the development of the first 4Runner sport utility vehicle. He came up with the idea in 1977, and in 1984 the 4Runner was introduced.

He loves his work and the most important part of it in John's opinion is "to be honorable, honest, and to tell the truth at all costs."

Without a doubt, he'll be in the automotive business for a long time.

It's Time to Plan Your Fall Garden

PV Style, September/October 1998

Even though Southern California doesn't have the seasonal changes that exist in other parts of the country, it is time to think about fall plantings. Bombarded by El Nino, overheated by unseasonably warm days and cool, damp nights, gardens might look a bit bedraggled.

The end of summer vacation may inspire some gardeners to think fall colors and new varieties of flowers. Bulb lovers may be thinking of a special spot for those colorful announcements of spring and summer.

Whatever your goal, now is the time to plan, plan, plan!

According to Larry Amling, Manager of the Armstrong Garden Center in Torrance, "There are three important steps: planning, preparation, and timing, but the most important is planning."

Palos Verdes landscape designer Julie Heinsheimer suggests if a major landscaping change is being considered, "Fall is the time to plant it."

Planning the garden involves deciding what kind of plantings will be included. If a combination of annuals, perennials, and bulbs is used, consider the growing time of each.

Mr. Amling recommends putting existing plants in place first, leaving a space in-between for the bulbs. In this way, there will be something blooming seasonally.

One may also leave an area strictly for a bulb garden, planting the bulbs in clusters. To enjoy fall color, potted plants may be temporarily placed in the empty spaces.

The important thing to remember is not to start too early. Think about timing and wait for the cooler period to plant in about the third week of September. One can enjoy the fall color in containers in the meantime during the warmer period, and then transfer them to their permanent location.

The Santa Ana conditions are always a consideration for the new color, so adequate watering is important. Any blossoms that die must also be cut out, followed by proper feeding. In preparing for new plantings, it's best to first clean out the old plants and growth.

Remove those that are at the end of the cycle. Cut back or remove dead blossoms from those plants with a longer growth period. Add a starter fertilizer that is lower in nitrogen and high in phosphorous.

The vibrant colors of the Iceland Poppies, a perennial used here as an annual, require full sun and brighten a dull spot in the garden. Flocks, Pansies, and Violas are other sun-loving choices.

Perennials including the double cushion-type Mums are hardy plants that come in a variety of fall colors. Hybrid Asters offer a color choice in pinks, mauves, and crimsons.

The showy Anemones are also a good choice. Calendula, or Pot Marigold, in orange, apricot, cream, and yellow, is long flowering. Perennials should be cut back after two to three weeks so they will flower again. Others such as low-water maintenance Lavender is a good fall choice, as well as Salvia.

In the shade family is the popular English Primrose, whose best planting time is about mid-October so that it will bloom through the winter. The Fairy and Baby Primrose with its broad leaves and vibrant color are perfect under a tree. The Cyclamen is another that will bloom happily in the shade through winter.

A dramatic large-leafed foliage plant is the Hosta. Available in several colors it prefers dappled shade and is a hardy, long-lived perennial. The fancy-leafed Caladium likes more moisture and looks best in groupings of color.

With so many choices for the fall garden, don't forget to plan, plan, plan, and you'll be happy with the results.

Restaurateur Entertains for the Holidays
PV Style, November/December 1998

Although the demands of restaurant life require that he be there each day, Cafe Cego's chef-owner Gerhard Moser knows it is time to think about the special dishes he will prepare to celebrate the holidays.

Thoughts of family, friends, and good food bring back memories of holidays together, and Gerhard enjoys recreating his German traditions for Christmas and the New Year. Growing up in the Black Forest region of Germany where both first and second Christmas Day are celebrated, pastry preparation begins "weeks ahead of time." The special desserts include Dresdnerstollen, Linzertorte, and special cookies including Lebkuchen and Nurnbergerlebkuchen.

Dresdnerstollen, a stollen unique to the holidays, is filled with dried fruits such as oranges, lemons, dates, and figs, as well as nuts and marzipan. Lebkuchen is a sugar-glazed cookie with hazelnuts, walnuts, and chocolate. Molasses, ginger, and raisins are the main incredients in Nurnbergerlebkuchen. Another specialty, Rhumtopf, is a dessert started in the summer when fresh fruit is at its peak. Kept "in a cool cellar" in a special ceramic container, the fruit is mixed with rum and sugar and left to ferment. New seasonal varieties are added as they ripen.

Christmas Day dinner "always" features goose with dumplings and red cabbage and Linzertorte for dessert. Christmas supper, a lighter meal, usually consists of black forest ham, salads, sour rye bread and, of course, more pastries.

Since Cafe Cego serves a special New Year's Eve menu, Gerhard and wife Bernice ring in the new year with their clients at their Rolling Hills Estates restaurant. New Year's Day is a quiet time at home during which they "watch the Rose parade."

Dinner, the most important part of the day, is shared with friends. The menu usually includes a game dish such as venison as well as beef and fish and a special dessert such as raspberry souffle.

Gerhard was born in Kuhbach, a twelve-hundred-year-old village through which the Romans passed on their way to Switzerland. He went to school in nearby Trieberg, where he began his chef's apprenticeship when he was fourteen years old. He has worked at his profession in Switzerland, Sweden, Mexico, and now Palos Verdes, where he lives.

He returns to his home in Germany every few years, where in the cellar he still finds special containers of schnapps and rhumtopf that were started in his youth.

Gerhard smiles and says, "I enjoy the traditions and the memories it brings back. That's why the special foods of holidays are so important to everyone—they recreate memories."

Hospice Foundation's
Jacky Glass Entertains
PV Style, March/April 1999

Jacky Glass, Chairperson of the Board of Trustees of Hospice Foundation, loves to entertain. She has done it in style each year when she acts as hostess for Sunday by the Sea, the fundraising event for Hospice. Held on the grounds of her beautiful home overlooking the ocean, the day offers tastings from fifty local restaurants and wineries. Last year, over 600 people attended.

What she loves best are small dinner parties for friends and family members, or lunch with tennis friends. She recently had a luncheon for the Sunday by the Sea committee and although she loves to cook, she often uses the services of a local restaurateur.

"They do so much for Hospice that I'm happy to support them as much as I can," Jacky says.

At such lunches, she will usually have a special salad as the main course, such as a Chinese Chicken, or Fried Chicken Salad.

"I make sure to include a fantastic dessert, because even those watching calories love a little sweet taste." One of her homemade specialties and personal favorites is carrot cake.

Jacky, born in Brooklyn, New York, came to California with CPA husband Jerry, who owns a management and development company in Orange County.

They have four daughters, one son, and five grandsons. When they get together with family, Jacky features a roast along with a favorite side dish such as a spinach noodle casserole and several desserts.

She might showcase her talents in Chinese cooking, which is her favorite. She once had an instructor come to her home who taught her and several friends how to prepare Chinese recipes. At the end of the lessons, Jacky created a five-course meal for her friends.

She also enjoys Japanese cooking. In her kitchen, built into a marble table, is a Teppanyaki. Used for Japanese style grilling, she enjoys demonstrating her skill at it, "but nothing like a Benihana," she says laughing.

Active in marine league tennis, she enjoys traveling and music, and used to be a member of St. Peter's by the Sea choir, "until my tonsils grew back." Now she combines her love of travel and music with visits to her daughter Jeralyn, who is an opera singer in Germany.

She is very proud of her involvement in Hospice. "We were one of only two hospice programs in the country at which the new Hospice postage stamp was unveiled."

Hospice also recently had its first annual Academy Awards Party. She looks forward to the ninth Sunday by The Sea event on Sunday, September 26th. All money raised goes directly to Hospice Foundation patient care.

"It's much work for everyone," Jacky says, "but at the end of the day, Jerry and I reflect about how wonderful it's all been and we're ready to do it all again."

YMCA's Chairman of the Board
Gerald Marcil: Advocate for Youth
PV Style, May/June 1999

One might say about Palos Verdes Estates resident Jerry Marcil that his business acumen started with a can of peanuts. When he was nine years old growing up in Torrance, he wanted to go to summer camp, but there was no money for him to do so. Someone at the YMCA suggested that if he sold a certain number of peanuts, they would match the rest with a scholarship. He met his goal, and the YMCA kept their promise. Today, he is Chairman of the Board of that very same facility, the Torrance/South Bay YMCA.

As President of Palos Verdes Development, Inc., this 46-year-old businessman is a highly successful, award-winning developer responsible for total sales of $136 million to date. His first encounter with the YMCA "left such an impression on me" that he describes it as the "most important experience in his life." He believes that his business philosophy, as well as his commitment to youth all stem from that beginning.

He remembers Gil Anderson, his counselor in the Trailblazer program, as "the most influential person in my life. I certainly learned morals and values from both Gil and the YMCA," Jerry explains. It is because of his appreciation that Jerry has made a large donation to the current YMCA Capital Campaign in Gil's memory. It was also in his honor that Jerry became a camp counselor at Camp Round Meadow near Big Bear when he was 37 years old.

Jerry later became Camp Director of the YMCA Surf camp for 12- to 15-year-old boys. He is currently a Junior Lakers coach, for a basketball program also at the

YMCA. He bought a 36-foot sailboat, learned how to sail, and now takes members for a twice a year trip to Catalina Island.

Jerry grew up in Torrance, attending North Torrance High School where he was captain of the wrestling team and became a California AAU champion. His parents always insisted that he was going to attend college, "so he had no choice." He thought then that he was an average student, but he graduated from El Camino College with an AA degree with honors. He then worked three years as a machinist and housepainter so that he could attend the University of Southern California. He graduated in 1976 with a BS degree with Honors in Business Administration.

After graduation, Jerry was going to open a bar and restaurant, but he had a real estate license, so he decided to try his hand at it. In three summers, he never sold one house, but in 1976, he did well during a six-month period and decided to try it for another six months. This continued until he became the top agent in 1979 on the Torrance, Lomita, Carson Board of Realtors.

In 1981, he completed his first development project in El Segundo and then developed the Tennis Club Condominium complex in the South Bay. In 1980, he created a property management firm and in 1982 created his current company. In 1992, when the real estate market downturned, he lost almost everything. From that, he learned that "one can only believe in oneself and family and friends."

Although his business is very important to him, Jerry's biggest commitment is to the youth. He was seeing "firsthand, kid's resignation and lack of interest in politics. They believed that what they had to say was unimportant; therefore, they were powerless to make a difference." This affected him so strongly that he did something about it. He formed a group called Foundation of America, whose mission statement says "by listening to, respecting, and integrating the voice and ideas of our youth, we can engage their fresh perspective and full potential for improving our nation."

In 1995, Jerry was told he had to "start small," but he knew the program had to be a national one. By making a personal financial commitment and through working with the schools, youth organizations, corporate sponsors, and enlisting the aid of individual board members, they established the Youthlink website.

Through the site, young people communicated their top concerns and suggestions for improving America. This led to the creation of the first Youth Convention concurrent with the 1996 Republican and Democratic Conventions. The youth delegates met with key national leaders, offering their National Youth Platform and calling attention to their "solutions for creating a better America."

Married to wife Carol, who he met at an awareness seminar, and father of three children, Jerry has no immediate personal goals, "He's happy with the way it is." He starts out each day, he says, "with a personal prayer. It is, help me be a good father, husband, friend, employer, businessman. Let me make a maximum positive difference and be a provider of your love and light to everyone I meet today."

His altruistic goals are to help the YMCA meet their $4 million building campaign, to work toward further empowering youth, and to have all Presidential candidates available at the next National Youth Convention. It appears that he indeed will make a maximum, positive difference.

Palos Verdes Review (1993-1994)

36th Annual
Rolling Hills Estates Celebration
Palos Verdes Review, September 1993

Rolling Hills Estates celebrated its birthday with an almost dawn to dusk party at the Empty Saddle Club and a good time was had by all.

Without a doubt, City Celebration Chairman Bob Riley saw to it there was something for everyone, and just about everyone was there to enjoy the events.

Townsfolk mingled with cowboys, cowgirls, sheriffs, hoofers, stompers, ropers, and line dancers. They petted horses, ponies, rabbits, sheep, chickens, and even a llama. They watched volleyball, played horseshoes, got their faces painted, danced, played games, took wagon rides and even "dunked" the sheriff.

And when they got hungry, what a choice! Western barbecue, steak, hamburgers, birthday cake, and more. If you missed it this year, be sure and mark your calendar for the 37th.

The Associates Hold Sunset
and Sand Party at the Beach Club
Palos Verdes Review, September 1993

A fabulous time was had at the new Palos Verdes Beach and Athletic Club when The Associates hosted a fundraising party to benefit the Palos Verdes Art Center.

Reservations Chairman Susan Boval greeted guests at the check-in table and designed the colorful invitations.

As the over 200 guests arrived, they were greeted by the sight of the fantastic facility in all its splendor.

Luminary candles led the way to the pool and terrace below, where Decorations Chairman Nancy Howell created table centerpieces of colorful beach balls and sand pails.

This set the fun tone of the evening that was Co-chaired by Pam Sherman and Associates President Carol Friedman. A wonderful buffet, dancing, and an auction led by *Palos Verdes Review* Publisher Ben Loughrin rounded out the evening.

Yule Parlor Parade— The Burnham Residence
Palos Verdes Review, October 1993

Each year Christmas arrives early on the hill when the Woman's Fellowship of the Neighborhood Church presents the Yule Parlor Parade. A popular tradition in its thirty-seventh year, hundreds of guests are expected to tour four unique homes on the Palos Verdes Peninsula. This year the tour will be held on Friday and Saturday, December 3 and 4 between 11 a.m. and 4 p.m.

In addition to viewing the festive splendor of the residences, visitors are invited to visit the restored sanctuary and the new Fellowship Hall at the church for tea and holiday music. At the same time, one may purchase gifts at the Bake Shop and Yule Shop.

Featured on this year's Yule Parlor Parade are the homes of Meg and Dan Burnham, Jacqui and Frank Campion, Ruth and Roger MacFarlane, and Tres and Ed Mennis. Pictured on the opposing page is the 5,000 square foot Mediterranean style residence of Meg and Dan Burnham, which will be decorated for Christmas Dinner.

Meg reflects on the fact that she and Dan have lived in eight states and have moved so many times during their marriage that, "you have to make every house you live in a home, but you have to do it quickly." She has always had an older more traditional house, and since this one was new, she wanted to do something to make it seem older. Her approach to interior design has usually been more conservative and traditional, but she says Vera Blakey of Inside Designs, "has really helped me to be more creative in my thinking and more daring. I would never have done anything like this before, but Vera's patience and her ability to help me see the outcome really gave me the courage to try."

As visitors approach the house along the Palos Verdes stone pathway, there is the expectation that one will certainly find something special behind the gaily decorated double doors, and one is not disappointed. The residence reflects the warmth and charm of the gracious owner who introduced herself by saying, "please call me Meg."

The walls of the entry are covered in hand painted wallpaper which has been torn into random shapes and applied to overlapping patterns to create a textured marbleized effect. In a prominent spot is an antique child's chair which was used by Meg as a little girl. It is covered in a needlepoint design created by her aunt. Flanking the double doors in arched alcoves are antique Japanese hibachis used as vases and filled with silk flowers.

Pictured is the step-up octagonal shaped living room; the curves of the arched, beamed ceiling influence the flowing outline of the silver-tone silk window treatment. A hand-painted border of a stylized vine encircles the room and creates a stylish signature on the antique glazed walls. A color palette of silver-grey, cranberry, blue, and accents of pale rose enhance the K'ang His coffee table of black cracked laqueur and the Chinese stacking tables.

Prominent in the room is a 1907 piano purchased in Buffalo, N.Y. during their stay there. "I had thought the children might be interested in learning to play, but they never did. However, we love it so much, we've kept it."

The dining room with traditional mahogany Federal Period furniture is counter-pointed with a high stainless steel effect wallpaper. A lighter metallic feeling is captured on the ceiling with a hand-painted wallpaper. The dining room will be set for Christmas Dinner with Duke of Gloucester china by Mottahedeh. The original was commissioned in 1770 by Duke William Henry and reflects his interest in the world of nature. The pattern uses nineteen colors and 22 karate gold.

Dan, president of Allied-Signal Aerospace, must often spend time working at home, so his office is made as comfortable as possible with an antique George II style mahogany inlaid desk with oval leather top. Meg and Dan are avid readers, and his office features a floor to ceiling bookcase built to house their large collection.

The open family room/kitchen area and its adjoining breakfast nook and butler's pantry offer whimsical touches including dog footprints in the Mexican paver stone floor leading to the dining room and a "Jersey" cow; a gift from friends in Short Hills, New Jersey from where the Burnhams moved. A print over the stone fireplace is suggestive, Meg says, "of their peek-view of Catalina." A collection of Shaker boxes with portraits of their former homes painted on the tops sit nearby.

Soft curved ceilings, interesting wall treatments, as well as unique furnishing and accessories make this a wonderful house in which to enjoy a Christmas dinner.

The Campion residence is a charming home designed by its owners and remodeled according to the design of

Frank and Jacquie's late son Robert. It features a collection of heirlooms assembled over a century by two French families. The focal point of the living room is a handsome armoire containing antique linens which are a dowry passed from eldest daughter to eldest daughter. Gracing the hall leading to the jewel toned master suite are oils by French painter Emile Delcourt. In the dining room at the opposite end of the hall are displayed pink porcelain pieces made by the Waldorf Astoria Hotel for the King of Serbia. They were left to Mrs. Campion by her late father, former "Maître d' extraordinaire" at the hotel.

Unusual furniture and accessories from South Africa highlight the home of Roger and Ruth MacFarlane. Featured in the entryway are Dutch tiles, paver floors, and an incredibly heavy teak bench from the Cape Town shipping office where Mr. MacFarlane's father sat as a messenger boy for the firm. Displayed on the walls in the remodeled kitchen are copper jelly molds and South African skillets.

One of the distinctive amenities in the home of Dr. Edmund and Tres Mennis is the use of Palos Verdes stone. Handmade furniture and beautiful Chinese hand-stitching is featured throughout. Displayed in a prominent spot in the living room is a set of handsome music stands, which Mrs. Mennis, a cellist, utilizes for her weekly "salons."

The Women's Fellowship, in their 37th year of planning and organizing the Yule Parlor Parade, have over the years used the funds raised from this event to benefit many charities. Among them are Toberman House, Harbor Free Clinic, Torrance YWCA, Meals on Wheels, and Hospice.

Palos Verdes Women's Club
Tea Guests Are Tickled Pink
Palos Verdes Review, October 1993

Pink and green balloons greeted arrivals and pink carnations were worn by past Presidents when the Palos Verdes Woman's Club held their annual tea at the spectacular Palos Verdes Estates home of Betsy Yarak.

While pianist Ada Belle Petterson entertained, Helen Gates, senior club President (1957) was among the past Presidents who poured tea for members and their guests. She also created the beautiful flower arrangements.

Among the popular events sponsored by the club are the Books & Authors Luncheon and the Garden Tour, their major fundraisers. Last year they disbursed $18,000 dollars to scholarship recipients and local charities. In addition, the club sponsors programs open to the public, at Malaga Cove Library.

CAP and Norris Theater
Celebrate 10th Anniversary
Palos Verdes Review, October 1993

The magic was CAPtured at the home of Julian and Caroline Elliott when the Community Association of the Peninsula had an elegant thank you party for its founders and early supporters. Jane Moe was Chairperson of the event. Moe and the late Agnes Moss were original co-founders. The celebration continued at the theater where partygoers had a buffet followed by entertainment.

CAP's activities include the Telethon fundraiser and Project Ego, a scholarship program for PV High School. The theater has a variety of support groups including Act II, Bravo, Chorus Liners, Encore Circle, and Friends of the Norris Theatre, and Friends—Japan Division.

Art for Fun(d)s Sake
Palos Verdes Review, October 1993

The 31st annual arts fair Art for Fund(s) Sake featured more than 100 artists who exhibited among jewelry, ceramics, and paintings.

Local artists who demonstrated their skills included ceramicist Richard McColl and weaver Dianna Brenna.

Art At Your Fingertips Renaissance Fair docents provided hands-on projects for the youngsters in the form of "flying machines" and coats of arms.

Entertainment and delicious food provided a respite in the day. Co-chairs were Corinn Bates and Gene Cantisano were event Co-Chairs.

Las Ayudas Holiday Preview
Palos Verdes Review, November 1993

Las Ayudas held their annual Christmas Boutique at the home of Diane Staes. Chairwoman Patti Dunst put together a hard-working committee to turn the residence into a gift-filled boutique of food items, decorations, and gifts.

Samples from their fantastic cookbook and their own blend of coffee were offered on the terrace.

The group of about 25 dynamic active members raises funds for a variety of charities, which this year includes Palos Verdes Art Center, Education Foundation, Community Helpline, P.V. Library, Neighborhood Alert on Drugs and Alcohol, and Hospice Foundation.

Western Hoedown in Malaga Cove Plaza
Palos Verdes Review, November 1993

The Malaga Cove Plaza Beautification Project hosted a Western Night fundraiser, the proceeds from which will help to create a tree-lined, pedestrian-friendly plaza.

Jere Murray, President of the Project, assembled a talented group to pull it all together, including Juan Forteza, who temporarily transformed the plaza into a frontier town. Co-chairs Sharon Ryan and Sue McNeil arranged the fantastic barbeque. The fun evening included casino games, line dancing lessons, pig races, and great country music.

League of Women Voters Holiday Party
Palos Verdes Review, December 1993

The League of Women Voters of the Palos Verdes Peninsula held their annual holiday party at Hesse Park Community Center to honor local elected officials.

The honored guests included city council members, library trustees, members of the school board, the Sheriff's department and federal and state representatives.

Co-chairs Jane Au and Shirley Borks oversaw a dynamic committee that included reservations chairwoman Lois Tarkington, refreshments chairwoman Donna Morton, decorations chairwoman Betty Schofield, and publicity chairwoman Doris Lasky.

New Year's Eve at the Norris Theater
Palos Verdes Review, January 1994

Betty Sevy chaired a spectacular Bravo evening at the Norris Theater where Vocalworks, a swinging classic jazz vocal group, entertained the black-tie audience. The guests then strolled across the street to the main level of the Shops at Palos Verdes.

Transformed into a balloon filled night club for the New Year's Eve champagne supper, everyone danced the evening away and welcomed 1994. Other committee members included Sophie Fitzmaurice, Joan and Dick Moe, Sal Intagliata, and JoAnn and Dick Evans.

Art Walk Features P.V. Peninsula Artists
Palos Verdes Review, 1994

The Art Walk is a self-guided tour that features the work of 21 award-winning Palos Verdes Peninsula artists. Presented by The Circle, a support group of the Palos Verdes Art Center, the walk presents a unique opportunity to view an extraordinary collection of work and the environments in which they have been created.

The one-day event will be held Sunday, March 20 from 10 a.m. to 4 p.m. An admission brochure will be provided at the time of ticket purchase and will include names and addresses of the exhibiting artists and a map to their homes/studios. This will enable guests to begin and end their tour where they wish and to select those whose work especially interests them.

This will be a hard decision to make since Co-Chairs Deedee Rechtin and Betty Wing have assembled a talented group of individuals who all have their own loyal followers and fans. Making the selection process simpler is the fact that the artists are grouped together geographically. Colorful markers in the form of windsocks will guide tour goers, and if one doesn't want to take time to eat lunch, light refreshments will be on hand at many of the stops.

The artists will be in their studios to greet guests and answer questions, and price lists will be made available for later purchases at the art center. The art center docents will act as hosts and provide additional information as needed.

All the artists included in the tour are exhibiting, professional artists with regional, national, or international reputations whose work is found in collections all over the world. They run the gamut from popular plein air artist Daniel Pinkham to the cutting-edge work of Janice Weisman's torso series and gauze-wrapped sculptures. Dan's work will be seen in his garden studio while Janice opens her home and patio for exhibition.

One of the longtime groups included on the tour are the "Summer House" watercolorists who have been meeting for ten years in the summer house of Carolyn Schaeffer to paint and critique their work. They include Joyce Bauman, Jesslyn Fain, Nicky Field, Helen Highley, Lois Hiler, Elaine Miller, Lura Newhouse, and Carolyn Schaeffer.

Deedee Rechtin, who is former program director at the art center, says that this group "represents one of the reasons the Palos Verdes Art Center was formed—to bring artists together."

Artists have always been attracted to the beauty of the Palos Verdes Peninsula as a vehicle for their art and a place to live, but it lacked a central place for artists to show their work and come together. Although early artists and groups met and exhibited their work at Malaga

Cove Library, they soon outgrew their surroundings. This produced the impetus for the creation of the Palos Verdes Art Center.

The Circle, which was established in 1975 as a social group, is now involved in the support of the center's exhibitions and education and community outreach programs. They also help to raise funds for the center through events like the art walk and the Cooks Tour, which alternate yearly.

This will be the third year that the group has produced the Art Walk. It will be the first featuring artists only peninsula artists, many showcased on the tour for the first time. Others, like Eva and Paul Kolasvary, have previously opened their studios. The Kolosvary's work includes assemblage collage and drawings. Their home features an outstanding collection of African and New Guinea art and showcases a lovely garden area leading to their work environment with a magnificent ocean view.

Another ocean view inspires the artistry of Leonard Rubenstein, co-curator of the Hi Tech-Low Tech ceramics exhibit shown recently at the center. He is a ceramic artist who creates sculpture and wheel-thrown pieces. Another ceramicist in a completely different vein is Pat Hinz, who does small replicas of local landmarks like Point Vicente lighthouse and the General Store.

The studios of Ruth and Gerhard Hanzlik are adjacent to each other and provide separate working environments for their individual approaches. Ruth is a sculptor who does both abstract and figurative bronze and terracotta pieces, while Gerhard's work involves portraiture and landscapes.

The studios at Margate School will showcase the mixed media of Anne Wittels and the visually exciting weavings of Mia Botts Zapp. Sherry Harris will be on hand to demonstrate the use of local, natural materials in unusual basketry.

Well-known water colorist Diane Clapp Bartz opens her studio for the first time. Her impressionistic work features many peninsula scenes. Jean Zaske's in-home studio and patio will also display scenes of the peninsula, but her technique utilizes a vibrant palette and bold strokes.

Other artists and their workplaces include the large studio of watercolorist Florence Strauss, mixed media artist Dee Henning's Garden spot, the garden studio of sculptor Pat Cox, and fiber artist Diana Brenna's home studio. The studio of Chinese brush painter Julia Tam and the residence of silk artist Judy Barnes Baker will be featured as well. Sara Austin's mixed media will be on display at her home studio, where Rita Kolas will demonstrate printmaking.

Meanwhile, there will be much excitement at the Palos Verdes Art Center, where a special exhibit of bronze sculpture and landscape paintings by Pulitzer prizewinner Paul Conrad will be shown.

Numerous demonstrations will take place throughout the day and refreshments will be served continuously.

Desert Writing (1999-2014)

Smooth Holiday Jazz Opens Theater
Desert Sun, November 26, 1999

Baby-boomers raised on Bob Dylan, the Beatles, and the Rolling Stones were just too hip for their dormitory rooms to be caught singing Christmas songs 30 years ago.

"Rudolph the Red-Nosed Reindeer," "Little Drummer Boy," and "White Christmas" were the domain of ancient, over-30 crooners like Gene Autry, Bing Crosby, and Frank Sinatra. Even Elvis Presley sought to appear contemporary on his 1968 "comeback" TV special by choosing to sing a song with social significance, "If I Could Dream," instead of the traditional Christmas tune his manager wanted him to sing.

But those same baby-boomers are expected to jump-start the holidays this week by attending two smooth jazz shows, one with a holiday theme.

Saxophonist Dave Koz, pianist David Benoit, guitarist Peter White, and vocalist Brenda Russell open the Festival of the Arts Theater in Palm Springs Monday in "A Smooth Jazz Christmas." Trumpeter Rick Braun and friends perform Saturday in La Quinta at the 1999 PGA West KJJZ Open House Jazz Festival.

Benoit, who believes he was one of the first jazz artists to make a Christmas album, says baby-boomers are ready for carols and traditional pop.

"(Baby-boomers) have more emphasis on family," said Benoit. "They want to feel good over the holidays but are tired of the same old music. They enjoy Christmas music, but in the same style and sound that they listen to the rest of the year. It's mellow music. It's hip, not corny or hokey…. Smooth jazz is a combination

148

of rhythmic sound and recognizable melody that hooks people in."

Jim "Fitz" Fitzgerald, program director and morning DJ at KJJZ, 102.3 FM, and a promoter of the Rick Braun concert, says holiday smooth jazz is enormously popular.

"It's a natural reaction from a generation that wasn't exposed to Christmas music," said Fitzgerald. "It's the instrumentation and groups the baby-boomers were familiar with that they are now introducing to their families. It's hipper. It's the sounds that they relate to."

The Koz-Benoit-White-Russell Palm Springs appearance is the ensemble's first in a 22-city tour. Their music is billed as "mellow traditional Christmas music with a contemporary flair." They'll do Christmas favorites and non-holiday pieces, such as Benoit's original "ReJoyce," showcasing the diverse styles of both headliners.

Nancy Dolensek, director of programming and development of the Festival of the Arts Theatre, describes her home opener as a "yuppie age-bracket concert." But she disagrees with the connection of the genre to any spiritual need.

"Every style of music, including jazz, pop, opera (and) classical has been applied to Christmas carols," she said. "To say that there is a certain age appeal because of just finding family values doesn't make sense."

Dolensek said she selected the Benoit-Koz team because it gives the theater its first trial run, "using every aspect of the house."

Benoit describes Koz as a "flamboyant (entertainer) who can ship the audience into a frenzy." Koz dances and interacts with the audience. Benoit gets his energy "from the piano." He sees their teaming as "an interesting symbiosis."

Joining Braun on his program are noted smooth jazz artists Gabriela Anders on vocals, Mark Antoine on guitar, and Brian Bromberg on bass guitar.

Braun and Benoit are old pals, having collaborated on Benoit's 1999 album "Professional Dreamer." Both find personal meaning in their compositions and in what they play. A favorite holiday song of Benoit's is "The Christmas Song," which he finds "complex harmonically." Another, "Santa Claus Is Coming to Town," is more up-tempo and he can "improv on it." "The Drummer Boy," one of Braun's Christmas album favorites, combines two or three different jazz elements to create a "festive sound."

Secrets of Spa Cuisine
Next, January 2000

Since cooking up flavorful dishes with little or no fat and making them look as appetizing as possible is a challenge that chefs at Coachella Valley's top spas face daily, we set out to discover some of their secrets.

Executive chef Miguel Morales and Chef de Cuisine Michael Catalano did "tons" of nutritional research before Fresca's opened in 1999 at the Marriott's Rancho Las Palmas Resort & Spa. Morales, who develops all the hotel's menus, admits that this was by far his "biggest challenge."

"Gourmet cooking with fresh, top-quality ingredients prepared in a healthy way with no oil and no butter," is the answer, he says. Most experts agree that no more than 10 to 20 per cent of calories should be from fat.

Morales and Catalano try to "set the standard on what spa cuisine is" by giving the customer "familiar food prepared in a healthy manner that tastes good and doesn't intimidate."

For instance, Morales, a graduate of the Culinary Institute of America, prepares a Sopa De Gazpacho with all the bursts of flavor found in the traditional sopa, but with no oil.

Although they have a spa, a large number of guests at The Spa Hotel & Casino in Palm Springs come to use the gambling facilities. "We have to please everyone," says Executive Chef Paul Woods, a Culinary Institute of America graduate. And, since the hotel is owned by the Agua Caliente tribe, many of whom have serious problems with diabetes and weight, Woods and Chef de Cuisine Tom Geike have developed many sugar-free dishes.

About 30 to 40 percent of items on the menu in the Agua Bar and Grill are identified as "health-conscious selections." There is a smaller spa cuisine menu as well, which identifies calorie count and fat grams.

Woods prepares a fantastic fat-free bouillabaisse-like dish called Ocean's Bounty, a mélange of seafood served around a bed of capellini in a tomato-Pernod broth. While typical pastas rely on a heavier dose of oil for flavor, the broth enhances the natural seafood flavors.

Lloyd's Light Pasta is so tasty, one would never know it has just a teaspoon of olive oil. It's prepared with whole-wheat linguine, garlic, chopped fresh tomatoes, diced chicken and basil and is 375 calories per serving.

The Ritz Carlton Rancho Mirage has a special menu available only in The Cafe. The selected specialties were designed under strict guidelines when the resort's spa opened three years ago.

They are "rich in carbohydrates and low in calories, fat, cholesterol, and sodium;" and are available at all Ritz-Carlton hotels.

They don't refer to it as spa cuisine, Executive Chef Phillipe Reininger explains, because of the connotation that it will be a "tasteless, boring, boiled" menu.

Instead, with his cuisine vitale, sushi-grade tuna, and other quality meats and produce, he emphasizes presentation along with "taste and light sauces" to appeal to the hotel's "sophisticated and cuisine-smart customers."

Small amounts of oil are used, while butter and cream are eliminated. He often uses natural reduction, a process used to intensify flavor by condensing the volume of sauce or broth by cooking over a high heat. Fish items comprise 30 percent of their menus, and meat, 60 to 70 percent.

The cuisine vitale items include dishes such as a lovely Two-Salmon Marinated Potato Salad made with smoked and fresh salmon, a fantastic Seared Ahi Tuna with Couscous Crust, and a light Risotto Primavera.

They have an outstanding repertoire of desserts that are as beautiful as they are tasty but may be a little higher in calories than most.

Operations Manager Mary Lou Rogers, claims The Palms in Palm Springs is "the only true spa" in the valley because it offers a "total regime of weight management with full spa menu."

Available only for their guests, the menu includes items such as a tostada salad and flavorful Sesame Stir-fry. Participants are allowed 1,000 calories per day with no more than 20 to 23 percent of those calories from fat. Red meat is replaced with chicken, turkey, and fish. And a delicious, cake-like chocolate truffle dessert is only 65 calories.

According to Tom Schnebly, food services manager, the philosophy is to provide clients with a nutritional, tasty, well-balanced diet that "offers the opportunity to lose weight, which they can follow if they so choose."

Chef Carl Hoover of Two Bunch Palms in Desert Hot Springs has no separate spa menu but features what he calls "health conscious" dishes. These include fresh, lean chicken or fish served with fresh vegetables, prepared without animal fats or butter. Since the spa attracts many vegetarians, Hoover caters to them with recipes like Vegetable Curry without dairy, and a Tofu Stir-Fry. Fresh fish is brought in daily, and meat is also on the menu.

The only spa desserts are sorbets and fresh fruit because most guests at Two Bunch "still want their cheesecake and tiramisu."

Valley chefs confirm their clients are more educated about eating, and "willing to try new things. There is also recognition that when the individual goes out to dine, "it's time to splurge."

So, there seems to be a push-pull attitude. They might eat the spa food, but still want a high-calorie dessert, or they may eat lightly during the day and let the night bring what it may.

Divine Decadence
Next, March 2000

If you are looking for a sensational dessert that is a feast to the eye as well as the taste buds, you don't have far to go.

The classic Baked Alaska with Strawberry Ice Cream and Caramel and Vanilla Sauce pictured above is the signature dessert at Wally's Desert Turtle, Rancho Mirage. Its creator, Limoges-born Jean Louis Jalouneix, explains that it is based on a classic French dish with adaptations. "I use strawberry ice cream, because I love it!"

Instead of the traditional square shape, the Alaska is a mounded tower of cloud-like swirled meringue, baked until the outer edges are golden brown. Airy puffs tipped with crispy ribbons of caramelized sugar melt in the mouth and leave a slight crunch on the tongue. Delightful counterparts include the silky fruit-filled ice cream and its bed of warm sponge cake coated with the dual sauces. The combination is so delicious that one's eyes close to focus on it. The deceptively simple array of ingredients belies the taste sensations evoked by this elegant, heavenly dish.

The Grand Marnier Souffle with Vanilla Bean Sauce served at Le St. Germain in Indian Wells is a testament to the traditional French souffle. It's served in individual ramekins and arrives at the table with a mushroom-shaped dome the color of a desert tan. An opening is made in the top, and much like releasing a genie from the bottle, a delicate puff of steam escapes. Along with it is the scent of vanilla and Grand Marnier. As the custard sauce is poured inside, fragrances mingle and permeate the air. Its lightness is a surprise to the tongue as the flavors meld with the smoothness of custard and the slight crunch of sugar.

The restaurant's most popular dessert, it reminds owner Michael Despras of the apple calvados souffles served at his home in Avignon, France where his great-grandmother owned two pastry shops. "People usually share it. It's romantic and also very elegant," Despras adds.

The Granny Smith Apple Dumpling with Vanilla Bean Ice Cream and Butter Pecan Sauce at Augusta in Palm Desert is also ambrosial. A nostalgic memory inspired the owners, Canadian- born artist Denise Roberge and her husband Larry Grotbeck, to develop this signature dessert in honor of Denise's grandmother.

"Preparing this dessert brings back childhood memories of crisp autumn weekends in New York State with my family," says Executive Chef Christopher Turini.

It is beautiful to look at, smells heavenly and makes one pause to admire its color and presentation. With the first mouthful, is a delightful array of flavors, temperatures, and textures. The apple center contrasts with light pastry wrap and crunchy sweetness of the sauce. Seasonal berries add textural tang. "We have prepared several thousand in the two years that we have been open, and it always brings a smile to our clients' faces," says Grotbeck.

The Dome Cake at Muriel's Supper Club in Palm Spring is another unforgettable confection. Its base of rich chocolate sponge cake, chocolate mousse, and caramel mousse center is glazed with bittersweet chocolate, decorated with edible gold leaves, and topped with a golden spun sugar cage. Like a beautiful, exotic creature, the creation is an amazing sight atop a bed of coffee sauce, and it's fun to ponder how to eat it.

As your fork cuts through the chocolate glaze, glides into the delectable mousse and gathers a morsel of the sponge cake, it brings out hidden macadamia nuts. The flavor is outstanding, but sweetness has been controlled with a light touch. Its creator, Executive Pastry Chef Ellen Yu, influenced by her training, European studies, and knowledge of food trends, has used America's love of chocolate to develop something unique.

Cuistot Restaurant in Palm Desert features a Raspberry Feuilletee with Raspberries and Caramel Sauce, a truly decadent combination. Created by chef-owner Bernard Dervieux, its inspiration is classic French training coupled with his American experience. "It's a beautiful dessert that's made fresh and put together with each order," says Dervieux.

The centerpiece of the dish is the feuillettee, layers of butter-filled puff pastry. One of the more difficult desserts to create successfully, it requires a delicate touch. Its success is apparent when the cream-filled delight is pierced with the fork to collect the cream, slightly tart berries, and warm, sweet caramel sauce. The tri-color presentation is a joy to the eye and its taste prompts a spontaneous moan of delight.

Starters From A to Z
Next, April 2000

Sampling a variety of fantastic appetizers is an economical and adventurous way to put together a tasty meal. For me, it's also a practical way to keep up with the latest creations of the valley's talented chefs, who offer everything from alligators to zucchinis on the starter side of the menu.

Le St Germain in Indian Wells, for instance, has a wide range of French selections and even offers separate starter menus. Fruits de Mer, individual choices of seafood appetizers ranging from oysters to abalone, is one of the most popular choices, says owner Michel Despras. The seasonal seafood platters in two sizes are also a great value. Le St. Germain Royal serves two to four people and includes assorted oyster, poached shrimp, raw clams, chilled steamed mussels, and a half Maine lobster. Le St. Germain Prestige, serving four to six people, includes the same with a whole lobster. Other popular appetizers are items such as Maine lobster ravioli, steamed black mussels, seared lump crab cake, sauteed sweetbreads, and wild mushroom soup.

A large assortment, both in choice and portions of Cal-Euro style hits is available on the menu at the trendy Palomino Euro Bistro in Palm Desert. "All our food is rustic comfort food, easily recognizable," says Executive Chef Tommy Criger. Appetizers like oven-roasted vegetable stromboli, spit roasted chicken pizza, Chop Chop Salad, oven roasted mussels, and grilled wild mushrooms, most enough for two people, are big winners.

The Vicenzo—cracked pizza crisps served with a trio of whole roasted garlic, creamy Cambozola cheese, and tomato chutney meant to be smeared en masse onto the crisps—is the top favorite. Next in popularity is the oven-roasted crab dip, a mélange of Dungeness crab, artichoke hearts, and Parmesan cheese served hot with giant pizza crackers. A bar menu available at special prices between 4 p.m. and 6 p.m. presents a separate selection and includes a few items from the regular menu.

Appetizing appetizers with a continental flavor in a beautiful setting is what you get at Wally's Desert Turtle in Rancho Mirage. Long-time chef John Louis Jalouneix is especially proud of the freshly made tartar of fresh tuna and his crab and lobster ravioli. Other starters, made daily in-house, are seared ahi with Thai slaw, Norwegian peppered smoked salmon, carpaccio of beef, Dungeness crab cakes, sauteed scallops and prawns, each with special sauces, and Sonoma foie gras. Caviar lovers have the luxurious choice of both Sevruga and Beluga.

Influenced by the tropics, Tommy Bahama in Palm Desert has concocted an exotic array of appealing little morsels. According to Restaurant Manager Kendal Tipper, "We're all about hospitality and we're delighted if a client wants to come in and just have the appetizers."

The tropical theme is represented by unusual items such as Bahamian conch fritters, Tommy's coconut shrimp, and Caribbean chicken skewers, which are tasty strips of chicken marinated in jerk seasoning, a spicy mélange of chili peppers. The interesting dips of tomatillo tropical jelly and ginger beurre blanc are a cool complement, and all go well with their exotic drinks. The Bungalow, a smaller menu, is also available in the attractive bar area from 4 to 5 p.m. and 10 to 11 p.m.

The Wilde Goose in Cathedral City offers daring samplers such as alligator tail and ostrich, along with their more conservative choices. The alligator is pounded thin and deep-fried. Filet of ostrich is charbroiled and served with a cognac-peppercorn sauce. Owner Wayne Weisbart says, "It's not unusual for clients to have several selections from the special menu as their dinner." Fresh Beluga caviar served with quail eggs, goose and pistachio confit, baked brie en croute, frog legs, cooked-to-order filet mignon chili, and ceviche provide other intriguing selections. If that's not enough, try Angel and the Beast: octopus simmered in a red wine sauce served over angel hair pasta.

The historical Palm Springs garden setting of Le Vallauris offers the Continental California touch to starters. According to owner Paul Bruggmans, "The seared crab cakes with baby greens in mustard mousseline is the most popular. "They're lighter because they're not fried and people like the combination of crab and whole-grain mustard sauce." Along with the recent addition of sauteed foie gras with apples and aged port, Russian caviar, croustillant of scallops with tomato, cumin, escargot, and house smoked salmon are just a few of the other lovely items presented.

Combining the traditional with the contemporary is the American style of Gila Steak and Seafood in Palm Desert. According to owner Anne Cannon-Le Pard, Executive Chef Chris Sizemore, newly arrived from Vail, "will be creating cutting-edge eclectic dishes, including great appetizers." The menu highlights a flavorful tiger shrimp quesadilla with mango salsa, Maryland style blue crab cakes served with chipotle remoulade and roasted sweet corn relish, and an unusual plantain empanada with fire-roasted tomato-chipotle sauce, one of Chef Sizemore's signature starters.

At Biga—The California Grill in Rancho Mirage there are starters on the regular menu as well as a monthly list of changing specials. You may be enticed by fantastic offerings like the Portabello ravioli, shrimp tortilla, crab quesadilla, grilled wild mushrooms, crab cakes with beurre blanc sauce, and Brown Derby Cobb Salad. Although larger than a starter, small plates—smaller portions of the entrees—are a special "bar only" menu. According to owner Michael Biga, "When I travel, I'm happiest eating at the bar, and it's the same for clients at my bar." Dishes include, among others, the large scallop and prawn Chinoise, petit filet mignon, and four chop rack of lamb.

No Mystery Chicken
Next, May 2000

When ex-detective Joyce Spizer entertains, the ingredients are plain and down-home good. It all began in Sweetwater, Texas where the mystery writer grew up. Living with her grandparents, she spent seven idyllic years learning how to cook and sew from her Grandma Foy.

That set the foundation for a lifelong romance with cooking and entertaining. When Spizer returned to Dallas to live with her parents, she added to her repertoire by reading magazines and cookbooks. She'd try out recipes, inviting guests to sample her fare. Like all cooks she had plenty of failures at first, but "I'd always have frozen chicken pot pies in the fridge, in case it didn't turn out."

For Spizer the secret to great entertaining is planning ahead. "I've had dinner parties at which I've cooked for up to 250 people. First, I plan my theme, colors, and decorations, and then the menu." She makes a list of what needs to be done, then assigns various tasks such as shopping, floral decorations, and serving to her support people. "It all comes together in a low-key, spontaneous way and looks like it just happened by itself." But without planning and organization, Spizer advises, "forget it, it won't happen."

The former detective agency owner recently had some Las Vegas casino executives as dinner guests. Among them was the casino's chef. Thinking about cooking for him made her nervous, so she fell back on her sleuthing instincts. She got the low-down on her guests' likes and dislikes. After this detective work, she decided on a more elegant affair than she'd thought up initially, serving chateaubriand with complementary side dishes. She had a glamorous dessert catered, a chocolate bombe with raspberries and cream. Her menu scored a big hit.

Spizer owns a large collection of colorful fabrics, table covers, and decorations of all types, and she continues to pick up items as she comes across them. She believes in making every event unique. For a Texas-style menu, she had her florist "look for some scruffy old cowboy boots, paint them and use them as a container for the floral centerpiece."

She'll go to great lengths to acquire food items she desires. She once lived alone on a farm in Oregon where she raised crops and did canning. She missed eating okra, a southern favorite, and was told by the locals that it was impossible to grow.

"I brought some back from Texas, planted it, put a screen around it; onions and radishes around that to keep the bugs away, and watched over it as it grew. Finally, it was ready to pick, but when I came out in the morning to harvest it, there was a deer standing in the middle of my okra and she'd eaten every bit of it. To make matters worse, it was a deer I had protected and fed."

Ms. Spizer now has a more urbane lifestyle than she did during her Texas ranch upbringing, but she still invests her La Quinta home with plenty of down-home warmth. And she opens her home up to friends and charities many times throughout the year.

The house is ideal for entertaining. Filled with artwork, it is open and airy (it was selected for the 1999 La Quinta Arts Foundation Homes Tour). "My husband Harold and I designed the house, and I designed all of the doors to reflect the desert and our life," she says, pointing out the mountain theme of the etched and frosted glass entrance door.

French doors lead to a back patio facing the golf course. The front patio houses the pool and spa, allowing for a natural flow connecting the outdoors with the inviting great-room, dining room, and kitchen. Each room is a unique entertainment area filled with comfortable seating and signature pieces such as the great-room's white baby-grand piano.

She is a party-giving veteran and knows how to show guests a good time. At a MASH party she and husband Harold gave a while back, the couple recreated a facsimile of the hospital unit complete with chow line and tin plates. Four hundred guests good-naturedly accepted the jibes of the "army sergeants, nurses, and cooks" who waited on them.

In another gesture of authenticity, the Spizers dug up their backyard for a Hawaiian luau where they roasted a whole pig. "We had quite a re-landscaping job after that event;' she says, laughing at the memory.

According to Spizer, "There are several things important to a good party. Use a caterer when your time is limited so you can enjoy your guests. Have the right mix of people. Don't overdo the alcohol and don't let the entertainment overpower the evening. Have a great menu and a theme."

With a new book, *I'm Okay, You're Dead*, coming out next month, Joyce Spizer won't be keeping up her usual entertaining schedule. She'll be on a publicity tour, and when she comes home it won't be to put her feet up. She's taken on the presidency of the Palm Springs Branch of the National League of American Pen Women, is involved in many other organizations such as

Soroptomists and Sisters-in-Crime and is working on a doctorate in marketing.

Ms. Spizer shares some of Grandma Foy's home-style recipes. A favorite dish, Grandma's Buttermilk Chicken recipe, "begins from the point where you catch the chicken who isn't dropping her share of eggs in the henhouse. Obviously, we don't do that anymore, but other than that the recipes are exactly as she told them to me."

The Art of Wedding Cakes
Next, June 2000

The wedding cake, once a rigid formula of tiered layers topped by traditional bride and groom figures, has evolved into an "anything goes" art form.

The latest design from H. DeVinn Visual in New York is a giant tower of chocolate frosted cupcakes, each decorated with multi-colored buttercream flowers. The cost is a staggering $3500.

Truffles, a bakery in Michigan City, Indiana, offers a decadent 16-layer cake with fresh Bavarian cream or buttercream, layers of fruit filling, and realistic paste flower decorations. The cake must be ordered nine to 12 months in advance of the wedding.

Atlanta baker Angie Bennett Mosier has created an antique garden urn cake meant to top a tiered wedding cake. It is made from rolled fondant filled with sugar paste flowers, fruits, and vegetables. It serves 15 and costs $800 to $1,000.

At the local level, Coachella Valley bakeries offer designs that range from artistic to traditional. Deborah Quinn, owner of the Pastry Swan Bakery in Cathedral City, says, "Lately I get more requests for abstract cakes that [look like] a piece of art."

Often the bride will bring in a photo of some Martha Stewart cake she would like Quinn to recreate using Quinn's specialty, a smooth-finish European rolled fondant sugar icing.

Quinn finds many couples moving away from bride and groom figures, preferring to crown their wedding cakes with either real flowers or hand-made sugar-paste flowers—designed to match the bridal bouquet, of course. The average price for a 3-tier cake serving 78 people is $350.

The most unique cake decoration Quinn has ever executed was a "mad hatter" cake in crooked tiers, using a color palette of bright oranges and yellows. The most unusual type of cake filling she's executed was a chocolate cake filled with chocolate chunks, crunchy peanut butter, layers of fudge, drippy chocolate ganache frosting, and big white chocolate curls on top—all of it displayed on staggered cake stands.

Adolf Ulbrich of Palm Desert's Chef Adolf's Bakery says that among his clients, traditional style is the favorite and chocolate the most popular flavor. He uses Italian icing frosting, a light mixture of egg whites, sugar, and butter. Another specialty, double fillings of freshly prepared Bavarian pudding with other combinations of fruit or chocolate icing, is often requested.

Fifty percent of his customers want the bride and groom figures on top. The rest want fresh flowers along with piped decorations. The average cost for a 3-tier cake is $225 to $245.

The biggest wedding cake Ulbrich ever constructed was as pastry chef at the MGM Grand Hotel in Las Vegas. It was a tower over 19 feet tall, with a base 12 feet in diameter. Covered with valence piping, there were 500 roses between the tiers.

The Orchard Bakery in La Quinta does a small volume of wedding cakes. According to owner Bill Fleet, they "keep it traditional, otherwise it's not cost-effective." For that reason, he turned down a request for a 750-piece cupcake cake tower. The largest cake he's made was four tiers four feet in height and held up on columns.

His biggest seller is a three-tier white cake with a lemon mousse filling, rolled fondant, or buttercream frosting topped with the traditional bride and groom figures. The average cost is $4 per person.

The most popular cake at Cathedral City's Carousel Bakery, according to owner Albert Cervantes, is a 10-tier sponge cake with fresh fruit filling, covered with whipped cream or buttercream. Fresh flowers are usually requested as decorations, along with the bride and groom figures.

Carousel also makes a "tres leche" sheet cake for weddings. A traditional Mexican three milk cake, it is made using regular, condensed, and evaporated milk. The average cake costs $1.40 per person and "I'll make any kind they want," says Cervantes.

Philippe Morlot, owner of Palm Desert's French Dessert Company, makes 200 to 300 custom wedding cakes per year. His most popular is made of layers of chocolate sponge cake, chocolate mousse, raspberry mousse, and fresh raspberries. It's frosted with ivory colored buttercream. Decorations are usually fresh flowers with added flowers of marzipan and lace of almond paste. Only a few customers want the bride and groom figures, "and I don't like to use it because it's too heavy for the cake," says Morlot.

His most unique cake served 1,000 people and consisted of 60 cakes shaped like gift boxes. He made 20 different exotic flavors such as pineapple, passion fruit, and lemon cheesecake, each with complementary fillings. Using alternating frostings of white icing, buttercream, and whipped cream, each was finished with a chocolate ribbon. The cost: $4500.

Summer Coolers
Next, August 2000

With summer's triple digit temperatures here, there's nothing like refreshing yourself with an old-fashioned iced treat. Cool choices await those searching for the perfect Coachella Valley confection, including such delectable delights as gourmet ice cream, frozen yogurt, and unique specialty drinks.

Award-winning Bert & Rocky's Cream Company in Palm Desert offers a truly decadent array of ice cream made on the premises. Owners Brent and Sherri Hunter have won four medals at the Los Angeles County Fair for their creative concoctions. Forty flavors are made on the premises in just 5-gallon increments—that's how fresh this ice cream is.

The most popular sellers, chocolate and vanilla, are made every day to two days. According to Brent, "our ice cream is the freshest in town. We are always creating new recipes, the ideas for which often come from our customers. An example would be our prize-winning nutty caramel coconut. It's coconut with lots and lots of nuts.

A good taste-tester is their sampler bowl—four flavors for only $2.50.

A long-time desert favorite is the delicious Date Shake. Tourists and locals alike find their way to Indio's oasis spots such as Shield's Date Gardens and Indio Orchards to enjoy the rich and surprisingly refreshing drink, which is unique to the Coachella Valley.

Chocolate lovers can check out Heminger's Fudge and Chocolate in Palm Springs. Owners Fred and Susie Heminger have been in the chocolate business since they were teenagers. "I've been making fudge since I was thirteen years old," says Fred.

When he was asked to make hot fudge sauce, he made it a tribute to their city in the form of the Palm Springs Ice Cream Sundae. It's a mouth-watering mound of three scoops of gourmet Dairygold ice cream, home-made hot fudge sauce, caramel sauce, whipped cream, and nuts, and is a bargain at $3.99.

Other favorites at Heminger's include the Root Beer Float, a taste-tingling combination of root beer soda with ice cream. One can also try the tangy Citrus Slam, a "secret" combination of orange, lemon, and lime juice. For an extra charge, you can get a "sipper," a cup with a built-in straw to keep you cool as you stroll.

Still searching for something novel to take the heat away? One of the bestselling ice cream flavors after vanilla at Haagen-Dazs of Indian Wells, according to District Manager Jon Molinaro, is the unusual Dulce de Leche, a sweet milk-based ice cream with caramel swirl. Originating in South American countries, it can also be had as a tastebud-thrilling split or milkshake.

An added plus at this shop is the wide array of exotic thirst quenchers. The Orange Dream Shake is as colorful as it is delicious. The luscious Moccachino contains a blended ice mix of espresso coffee, chocolate syrup, milk, and ice cream topped off with homemade whipped cream. Tea lovers can enjoy the sweeter Iced Chai Latte, an Indian tea base ice-blended with steamed milk, ice cream, or yogurt.

Fresh fruit smoothies here are a fruit lover's dream. Made with the natural ingredients of fruit, fruit sorbet, and non-fat yogurt with flavors such as berry, mango, and orange-mango, they are mouth-watering refreshers. You might want to skip dinner on a really hot evening and go straight to a chilled dessert. The Carmel Pecan Fudge Sundae and the Toffee Crunch Tartufo are meals in themselves at California Pizza Kitchen in Palm Desert and Palm Springs.

Do you have special dietary needs? Goldmine Yogurt, a popular shop in Rancho Mirage, always features eight flavors of delicious dairy-made yogurt: one that's sugar free, and the rest either low-fat or non-fat. According to owner Mark Boris, "I've always dreamed of providing a place where people could come for a high-quality, healthful treat."

Manager Wanda Reed reports that some clients, told about the shop by their doctors, get "almost teary" to be able to enjoy a treat previously unavailable to them.

The most popular flavor is peanut butter and if they sell out, she says "people are really upset." A small size is a generous eight plus ounces and sells for under $2.00, probably one of the desert's best buys.

Palm Springs' newest ice cream treat is Coldstone. The ice cream is made on the premises, and according to owner Thomas Gillespie, "It's the freshest ice cream you'll ever have unless you make your own."

The unique feature at this fun spot is the "mixers." The chosen flavor of ice cream is mixed together on a marble slab with additions like chunks of the most popular item, Reese's Peanut Butter Cups, or others such as nuts, Heath Bar chunks, M&M's, jellybeans, and many more.

One customer chose 21 things to be added to his ice cream, "at an extra cost, of course," says Tom.

Dining With the Peanut Gallery
Next, October 2000

Now that school has started, finding fun places where parents and kids under 12 can dine together is a top-priority item. We've come up with a few worry-free suggestions.

Chuck E. Cheese's in Palm Desert is probably the ultimate fun-time spot. A great place for celebrations of all kinds, it provides a safe and comfortable, although high-energy, atmosphere. Not your typical pizza parlor, it's a place where parents and kids can wear themselves out with games of all kinds, before or after they eat.

A menu is posted with a variety of package prices. The best deal, the Family Saver, is geared to a family of four and includes an extra-large pizza, four soft drinks and 100 game tokens for $35.99. The pizza is quite tasty. It arrives good and hot, with a well-browned and crispy crust and, of course, a choice of toppings.

If you're not the pizza-lover in your family, there's always the salad bar: limited but fresh selections at $3.99. There's also a tasty, towering sub-sandwich, served with French fries for $4.49, and the ever-popular hot dog with all the trimmings at $2.19.

The outstanding feature of this dynamo dining spot is that kids can't enter or leave without an adult. Your darlings can have a reasonable run of the place while you sit in a comfortable booth, able to observe them at all times.

General Manager Robert Ramirez says, "Families enjoy themselves here. They average a stay of one-and-a-half to three hours."

McDonald's playlands in La Quinta and Indio offer similar merriment on a smaller scale. An indoor playground for children under four feet tall with slides and colorful tubes for kids to crawl through are the energy-busters here.

The Indio restaurant also has game machines for the older kids. The choice of the day is the ever-constant Happy Meal which, at $1.99 to $2.39, is a bargain. The kids not only get their burger, fries, and drink, but also the toy of the moment.

Many family restaurants have special menus for the little ones. Among these is Red Robin in La Quinta, as colorful as its name. A small video game room near the front door provides diversion if a wait is necessary.

General Manager Paul Austin says, "Here, kids are our main client; they bring the adults."

The main room has a full-size carousel horse as a focal point. The tables and booths provide comfortable and attractive seating with good lighting. Once seated, the placemat-menu and crayons keep youngsters busy while waiting for their food.

For kids 10 years and younger, each item is $3.99 and includes steak fries and a beverage served in a plastic take-home cup. In addition to the goodies mentioned earlier, they can choose from Cheesey Mac'n Cheesey, Carnival Corn Dog, Lil' Guy Fish, and Jr. Clam Strips. Everything here is served in a basket, which kids seem to enjoy.

Adults and older children have a huge menu of choice with everything from seafood dishes (such as the large basket of clam strips with fries, described as "eating ecstasy"), to an exhaustive selection of burgers: turkey burgers, chicken burgers, meatless burgers, fish burgers and a selection of classic and gourmet burgers. All are served with unlimited steak fries and range in price from

$5.95 to $7.85. Monster Shakes, actually a shake and a half with a refill on the side, are also good values.

Kids of all ages and the young at heart are happy at California Pizza Kitchen in Palm Springs and Palm Desert. There are a variety of tasty treats on the regular menu that have been adapted to a kids-under-10 menu of yummy pasta and pizza treats.

"Kids really love the curly pasta-fusilli," says Palm Desert Manager Eric Richter.

For $4.99 kids get a choice of three different pizzas, or fusilli pasta in five versions, including the melted butter sauce so many little ones seem to love. Included is a refillable fountain soft drink, lemonade, or milk.

For 50 cents more, they can get a triple-thick fudge sundae or an old-fashioned brownie with chocolate sauce and whipped cream. Crayons are given with the menu to keep young minds amused.

Another perk is a fill-out card for the birthday club: when that time of year rolls around, the restaurant sends kids a card good for a free meal. Older ones in the crowd have a diverse selection of wonderfully fresh thin-crusted pizzas with a myriad of toppings, a wide range of delicious pastas, and soups and salads including everyone's favorite, Oriental Chicken Salad.

Mexican restaurants like Las Casuelas Nuevas in Rancho Mirage and Las Casuelas Terraza in Palm Springs are great for kids, since the regular menu includes a large selection of foods they like, such as tacos and burritos.

Parents can enjoy more sophisticated treats such as Cilantro Chicken Salad and other ethnic and continental dishes. Both spots have patio dining, which lowers stress levels for parents, and both have kids' menus.

At Rancho Mirage on Sundays there is a buffet of festive selections with a reduced price for children. An added plus at both places is the mariachi music, which gives everyone a lift and adds to the enjoyment of the food.

At Hometown Buffet in Palm Desert, the $6.78 lunch and $9.15 dinner include everything from soup and salad to desserts and beverages, all prepared on the premises. For kids aged two to 12 years, prices are only 50 cents multiplied by the age of the child.

Families and children really seem to enjoy themselves here. The atmosphere is casual and comfortable with a friendly, welcoming staff. Since food is prepared in small batches for freshness, the colorful, home-style buffet islands are replenished regularly with a variety of goodies.

One night a week is barbecue night, featuring beef ribs, country fried steak, chicken and hand-carved ham and roast beef. On Sunday nights, carved turkey, roast beef, and ham are showcased with all of the trimmings.

Saturday is especially geared to kids, with fun items like hot dogs and toppings, mini corn dogs, corn on the cob, macaroni and cheese, chicken, and spaghetti and meatballs added to entice little appetites. A beverage fountain serves regular or chocolate milk as well as other popular refillable drinks.

The dessert bar is every kid's dream: goodies from warm cherry cobbler like grandma used to make, to rice Krispy bars, cookies, cakes, puddings, and soft ice cream.

A true '50s landmark is Keedy's Fountain & Grill in Palm Desert. Complete in every retro detail including Formica counter and tabletops, the walls are covered in collages of old movie posters and photos. It's fun to sit at the counter on the old dining stools and watch the waitresses make delicious sodas, sundaes, shakes and floats at the old-fashioned soda fountain.

The menu has all the comfort food that kids and big folks enjoy: hamburgers, BLTs, chili, and a terrific selection of specials such as meatloaf, enchiladas and other favorite items.

Breakfast is served all day, so pancake-loving kids of all ages can satisfy their craving and have them for lunch or dinner.

Speeches

Resident Explores Family History Through Old Ohio Frontier Letters

By Dana Klosner, *Palos Verdes Peninsula News*
Saturday, October 29, 1994

Peninsula resident Jacqueline Bachar sat in her beautifully furnished living room overlooking an astonishing ocean view and told the tale of her ancestry. An invitation to a luncheon honoring a former first lady adorned the wall of this influential family's home. But the tale she told was of a poor 19th Century woman.

Bachar, originally from the East Coast, always had the urge to research her family's history. But her research began in earnest when she came home from living in Europe after the death of her mother. Her knowledge about her father's background brought her to the Lackawanna, Pennsylvania Historical Society. What she found was a first-person account of a woman's life on the Ohio frontier, ripped from the bosom of her family, and struggling with hardships.

The tale vividly came to life for Bachar when she discovered personal letters written by her great aunt eight generations back, to her brother, Deacon John Phillips. *Life on the Ohio Frontier: A Collection of Letters from Mary Lott to Deacon John Phillips, 1826-1846,* has made this collection available to the public. This is the first publication of newly rediscovered correspondence between a long-separated sister who was removed from New York State to the Ohio frontier, and her older brother in Pennsylvania. The letters contain a poignant description of life on the frontier. They are written with great expression and include moving exclamations of a strong religious faith. The letters serve as a wonderful glimpse into American history, and an astonishing account of women's roles and tribulations. Many informative references to family and friends of general interest as well as to those descendants of individuals are mentioned.

"These are the writings of Mary Lott," Bachar explained. "She was the sister of my Revolutionary War grandfather Deacon John Phillips. He was 30 years older than she and they were separated from each other when she was a child. Therefore, she refers to herself as a 'child of sorrow.' They had the same father but different mothers. As was the law at the time of their father's death, she was appointed a guardian and removed from the area, the location unknown. It is known there were other children as well, also separated from each other."

Lott was a woman of great fortitude. She faced illness, poverty, hardship, and other sufferings. But she endured. Her spirit was undaunted. She missed her family a great deal, as every letter revealed. She persevered. Her faith guided her through. Always sure that if she wasn't fortunate enough to have the opportunity to see her loved ones again in this life, she would see them in the next.

Lott talks of making linen by hand, and the family business of making sugar. She talks of close friends' illnesses and deaths. Life was precious and fragile in those times. Every letter expresses her gratitude that her brother and family are living, and she is just as grateful that she and her husband's health are "common."

The letters were saved by another relative of Bachar's, Hulda Brown, who was researching the family history in regard to land ownership.

After her death, Brown's collection was given to the Historical Society. The "collection" was composed of boxes and boxes of notes written on a variety of scraps of paper, including the backs of bills and receipts. It was in one of those huge, unorganized boxes that Bachar came across the handwritten copies of Mary Lott's letters. Bachar's book has generated interest from many Women's Studies programs at junior colleges and universities throughout the country and internationally. She has even been contacted by University College in Galway, Ireland, where the Women's Studies program is in its infancy.

Bachar found through her research that she is distantly related to Elizabeth Cady Stanton, who founded the women's movement with Susan B. Anthony.

"This is where it gets really exciting," women's activist Bachar said. Bachar had been involved with the National Council of Women, which was started by Stanton and Anthony.

"When we trace far enough back, we find we're all related," Bachar said.

Letter to the Editor
Palos Verdes Peninsula News, November 5, 1994

To the Editor,

Many thanks to Dana Klosner and the *Palos Verdes Peninsula News* for the wonderful article about my book, *Life on the Ohio Frontier: A Collection of Letters from Mary Lott to Deacon John Phillips, 1826-1846* (October 29, 1994). She did a wonderful job in capturing the essence of the difficulties facing a woman on the frontier.

I would like to call attention to the fact that my book is available for sale in the gift shop of the Peninsula library since any purchases made there benefit them. I would also like to express my appreciation for their continued support of local authors.

When my ancestor Mary Lott died, she had only two Bibles and six books in her possession, her entire collection. We have the luxury of thousands of books in wonderful libraries in our community.

I look forward to the time when their collection continues to grow, and all libraries will be operating full time again.

Jacqueline Bachar
Rancho Palos Verdes

Mary Lott, Child of Sorrow
National Council of Women, November 17, 1994

My presentation today will concern my book, *Life on The Ohio Frontier; A Collection of Letters from Mary Lott to Deacon John Phillips 1826-1846.* It is very rare to find such a collection of letters that spans a period of twenty years. They are a wonderful description of life on the frontier and the stories of Mary, her husband Henry, and Mary's brother Thomas.

My book is a tribute to Mary's memory. Her letters describe a frontier existence no different from that of the men in her life. She was equal partner in the hardships and drudgery of everyday activities and was often expected to go beyond what we may think of as her fair share of the load. She appeared, however, to be a true partner to her husband Henry, and in many examples in her letters appeared to be the decision maker. As I talk to you today, I would like to relate some historical points to some of the events Mary referred to, particularly as they influenced her in her early life and later life in the wilds.

In her first letter of October 8, 1826, Mary gives many details that really don't tell the whole story of her journey. She says, "We came from Buffalo to Portland on the steamboat, had good luck, was two days and two nights on water, but we had a very tedious journey from there in consequence of rain and new roads. We found it about 100 miles." The fact is that life's rules of conduct were quite controlled, particularly for women.

In the 1820's, new transportation modes like steamboats caused new expectations of behavior. There were various attempts to segregate the sexes, both on board and in waiting rooms. While traveling on a steamboat, an English woman writer of the period describes the men's cabin on the boat as the more desirable, writing that, "their exclusive right to it is somewhat uncourteously insisted upon." She also described the fact that husbands and wives were separated throughout the entire journey and could only be together at mealtimes. We can assume that Mary, her husband, and brother had to comply with these rules.

Mary describes their difficult Ohio beginnings by saying quite simply, "...we have bought fifty acres of entirely new land joining Leonard's (Henry's brother). Got two log rooms raised." In another letter, Mary refers to their financial difficulties when she says, "there was $54.00 behind on our place we did not get. I think, in consequence of not taking my advice. The man came for the deed. I told Henry not to give it up till he got the money, but the man said he should have it next day. We waited two weeks, could not get it—had to come away suing the note and leaving the business with Anson Williams." Women were normally excluded from business decisions, but it is obvious that Mary had a better sense for good business arrangements than Henry. At today's present value, the money they were owed is worth about $10,000.

Mary was probably born about 1782 in the Wyoming Valley in Pennsylvania, the frontier where her father Francis had emigrated. When he died by 1791, English and Colonial law still influenced life. After a husband's death, a widow was not allowed to be guardian to her own children after they reached a certain age if ownership of property was involved. The mother could not oversee it. Also, the death of a husband often necessitated selling the homestead to pay off his debts. A mother might then be forced to send children to other families as bond servants if she could not afford to keep them. In these instances, a guardian would be appointed by the court or selected by the child. In Mary's case, a record of her selection of a guardian is noted in 1796 in the probate records of Luzerne County, Pennsylvania, in which she was described as a "minor over the age of fourteen."

It is not known where Mary spent her younger years, but when discussing mutual family friends in a letter, she relates, "Abraham says the tender tie of friendship felt for me in childhood when I was separated from all relatives are yet the same, and although we have been separated so many years, yet he believes with you and me that time or distance can never break those tender ties of friendship." An unhappy childhood is hinted at throughout her writings when Mary refers to herself as a "child of sorrow."

Mary's strong religious faith is apparent throughout her letters. Faith is verbalized in many other diaries and letters written by frontier women. It is interesting to note that after the American Revolution, church attendance decreased due to the new separation of church and state. With exceptions, it remained in decline throughout the country. However, during the first quarter of the Nineteenth Century, churches made a concerted effort to widen membership. Finding that males were less influenced in daily life by religion than females, ministers recognized that faith was of immediate concern to women. Some scholars suggest that the women, although accepting of men as church leaders, learned that there were few places outside the home other than the church where autonomy was allowed and accepted, and therefore religion came to be accepted by men as woman's realm (Clinton, *The Other Civil War, American Women in the Nineteenth Century*).

To the women on the frontier, maintaining Protestantism was one of their greatest challenges. It satisfied their spiritual needs and explained their daily life: all things were "the will of God." Evangelical revivals gave women the opportunity to take control and be given essential roles. Participation in camp meetings and revivals gave women the opportunity to become leaders and charismatic figures in their own right. But the most important aspect for women was the socialization and feelings of security they provided through the woman's relationship with other women.

Mary's interest and involvement is expressed when she writes, "the inhabitants appear very friendly, and meetings handy of almost all kinds, though no particular revivals of religion at present." In another letter, she says, " it is most meeting time and I must omit some things I would have wrote, for I should have wrote finer had I not been in such haste..."

Historians say that the Presbyterian religion was "among the best organized in Ohio" (Knepper, *Ohio and Its People*). In describing one of their meetings, Mary says, "The Presbyterians have had a protracted meeting and it lasted almost two weeks, nite and day. There was near forty moved forward and about twenty professed to obtain a hope in Jesus. May they ever stand fast in that Liberty where with Christ has made them free."

In the 1830's the issue of the abolition of slavery became a natural outgrowth of women's domestic and religious life and was a precursor to women's suffrage. Mary's brother John apparently had strong opinions regarding this issue, as did Mary. In a letter dated 1838, Mary writes, "We return you many thanks for your papers. We think them very good and their opinion on slavery exactly with my mind, for ever since I come to years of understanding, I believe slavery a great evil and an abomination in the eyes of our Heavenly Father, and for such enmity to be suffered in a nation that has been so cried up for a land of liberty. And I do believe if something is not done soon to alleviate the sufferings of the poor slaves, that the Lord will deliver them as he did the children of Israel some way or another, and as a nation we shall be scourged, for the beautiful true liberty [will] no more flourish, for the limbs are already loped and the leaves are withering."

Communication with family and other women friends was important. The commonality of Mary's pleas for family to move to the frontier is seen in other examples of women's writings, and if they couldn't get relatives to move to the frontier, then there were always plans to be made to visit the old family home. Concerns about feminine appearance and proper clothes are also prominent among writings. Mary shares her worries when she writes, "I shall try very hard to come, if we all have our health and can possibly get a little spending money and a few clothes that I think you will not be ashamed of me."

If family or friends couldn't come or visits couldn't be made back home women had faith that relatives and friends would still come together in Heaven. This belief sustained them as it did Mary. After a disappointment of not being able to make a trip to Pennsylvania she writes, "my determination is to see you, should the Lord spare our lives and health. And my prayer is, that Jesus may be your best and dearest friend, and support the tottering frames till we meet again in this life, but if not here, I fully believe we shall in Heaven when this short voyage of life shall end."

I would now like to read a complete letter that describes several of the conditions I have discussed and shows Mary's struggle with anger, disappointment, sadness, and her desire to keep her faith and show forgiveness. It is a dramatic letter written August 7, 1829. Mary has now been in Ohio for about three years. There is a period of two years between this and the last letter she wrote. In the previous letter dated July, Mary expresses her worry about the fact that she hasn't heard from their brother Cornwell, who is supposed to be on his way to Ohio. She's in a bit of a panic because she doesn't understand what has happened. She says they can't live alone much longer at their ages, and then receives a letter from John telling her that Cornwell is not coming. This is her response.

Dear Brother & Sister,

I received your kind and affectionate letter this morning and amidst a thousand cares and a heart filled with sorrow and disappointment, I lift my pen to acknowledge my gratitude to you for the favor you now sent in addition to the many others I have received from your dear hand. I rejoice to hear that you are yet alive and in common health and likewise all your posterity. But the information you gave me concerning Cornwell [Phillips] fills us with sorrow and disappointment. How can I bear the thought that my dear brother should have no more stability than to sell and give us encouragement and then squander away his money and not come. The disappointment is great! And Henry feels as bad as I do.

We have both worked like dogs to get all we could to help them when they come. I told you in the letter put in the Post Office the day you wrote yours, how much corn we had planted. It looks well. We have got our wheat in the barn. It is very good. We shall [have] about 70 bushels. We have potatoes plenty for two families. Our flax is pulled and stacked. We shall have about 100 weight. We have saved 30 weight of our old on purpose for Esther to spin before the others got rotted. I have got a loom wove-two pieces, and got another in. I meant to have learn't Esther to weave *[Ed. note: Esther was probably Cornwell's daughter]*. We have lost no creature since we have been here, but a hog last winter. But, however, we have 21 big and little which we thought would be enough to fat for both families.

I should have anticipated on enjoying some happy hours with them, had I not known I was born a child of sorrow and misfortune. Disappointment always awaits me, yet I would sometimes look on the fair side of the leaf and think from the encouragement he gave us, he would come. But alas, I must now give up all hopes and to whom shall we look to smooth the moments of our declining years.

We have worked hard all our lives, but hard fortune was always our companion. The Lord in his good providence has never been pleased to give us a great stock of this world's goods for which I feel to bless his name. For if he had given me much of this world's riches, I might not have laid up my treasures in Heaven. Then I should have had my heart fixed on these low grounds where sorrows always grow. But now, dear brother, in the midst of adversity and disappointment, my soul beats high with anticipation of soon outriding the storm of affliction. Although I may never meet some of my dear friends in this world, yet, I think I have a hope that is sure and steadfast and reaches to that within the veil.

That I shall meet my dearest friends that never fails on the other side the cold streams of Jordan, where I shall enjoy His presence without a dimming veil between.

When I first read your letter, I thought I hardly knew how to be reconciled to this heavy disappointment, but a thought soon struck my mind. That was, trust in God. He will supply all your wants. I thought that notwithstanding, we were not rich. We had enough to support us through this short journey of life and what do we want more the next. And always as long as we live alone, we must work very hard and always be confined and should we live and die, so we should leave just enough for his relation to quarrel about. Henry says that they have got enough, that he has worked hard. Someone must be found that we can depend on if possible and we do believe there are such ones.

Now brother, do you think there is any of your grandchildren that would come, that we could depend on? My mind pitched on James Tripp. I liked him and his wife very much when I was there. I thought by his talk he had some notion of coming to this country or some other. If you think he would come, we want you should talk with him. Tell him he shall have the same chance [Cornwell] was to have. If he could sell and bring his money, he could buy land to a great advantage. Our little place would be a good home for them.

But, however, we shall leave it altogether for you to choose. I don't know as you will think you can spare any of them, but as you have so many, I think your heart cannot withhold should any of them have a mind to come and smooth the last moments of a poor old Uncle and Aunt. Write immediately and let us know. We shall wait till we get another letter before we look out for anyone else. But Henry says, they must come this fall or beginning of winter. Don't disappoint us again, for we can't wait any longer. We must know as soon as possible that we may know how to calculate our affairs and to lay in provisions for them. I shall flatter myself once more of having some one of my relatives with me in a strange land, but perhaps these hopes are only raised to be blasted again, but I feel to submit to Him that does all things well.

Dear brother, I hardly know what to tell you concerning my going to see you. My heart says I must go and once more embrace my dear old brother and sister. I often regret the time you mention in one of your last letters, but in vain. We can't recall past time [if it] had [not] come [as] welcome as we expected... I think if we had our health as well as we have had, that one or both would have went this fall. I will hope yet if anyone should come from there, that would take care of the things and Thomas, we might come yet this winter. If Henry could not go with me, I should venture to go without him if I could get a chance and I think there is a probability of it. There is always a number going in the fall.

You can't think how bad poor Thomas felt when he heard that Cornwell was not coming. He had black walnuts laid up for the children, would talk about them every day as he and I was pulling flax. He would say next year, Cornwell's little boys will help me and how much comfort he should take working with them, but this conversation has come to an end.

He is still my brother. I still love him as such. He has the same place in my heart. I still feel the same ties of natural affection. He shall have my prayers that notwithstanding he might have erred in judgement. My earnest prayer is that he may seek an interest in Christ and be [a] partaker of that pure and undefiled religion before God the Father, which will bring us still nearer by the blood of the lamb.

While writing, my heart sinks within me. Oh Cornwell, had I been there when you had your sixty dollars and yoke of oxen, I think a sister's entreats would have availed and you would have come, for when I think how much better it would have been for you and your family, as well as us, I hardly know how to be reconciled and sometimes reflect on myself for ever requesting you to come. For it appears that it has been the means of your selling yourself out of house and home, but one thing I have for consolation, a clear conscience. I meant right and thought it would be best for both and had not the least thought that you would sell and give us such encouragement and then not come, but if I never see your face again in this world of woe, you shall have my love and best wishes and likewise your wife and children.

Tell Esther, I had flattered myself much with the idea of having her as well as the rest to wait on me, should [I] live to old [age]. My hopes are blasted, but if I see none of you more, I hope I may see you all in Heaven, when the storm of life shall end. I expected you would have written to me when you found you were not coming but let nothing stop your correspondence. Write immediately and I will answer you.

Your affectionate sister Mary Lott.

The remaining letters cover the period up to 1846 and are filled with descriptions of Ohio, their work, moments of happiness, illness, death, and faith. They are always filled with longing and loneliness. The poignancy of the life of frontier women is described by another writer who says, "clinging to a few treasured heirlooms as reminders of a kinder life, they accompanied their husbands, ...suffering the most desperate physical hardships as well as a desolating sense of loneliness. Mary's loneliness and despair become more apparent as the years pass and at the end, she is without family members.

After Mary's husband Henry's death, as was required by law, an inventory of possessions was taken. Included, along with a description of farm implements and a short list of household items, were Mary's two spinning wheels, her loom, two bibles, six other books and, incongruously, one red fan. A memento from a happier time and place, it evokes a vision of a young woman filled with hopes and dreams moving forward into the future. As we read her story told through her letters, her trials and tribulations may fill us with the sad recognition that her life of hardship was shared by many other women who were carving a path in the wilderness for us to follow.

We should not think of Mary as a tragic symbol, though. Rather she was a woman of strength, courage, and faith. Her life should be considered a proud tribute to all the women who went before and came after clutching and cherishing their own red fans.

The Red Fan
Lackawanna Historical Society, March 29, 1995

I'm so excited to see you all here, and the first question I would like to ask is, I'm wondering how many of you am I related to, the Millers and the Phillips? Can I see a show of hands? I already know some of my family, anyone else related to the Phillips? Great.

I think I'm related to just about every family in the town. But anyway, really, it's just lovely to see you all here. I'm absolutely pleased that you have invited me here to speak to you members and guests of the Lackawanna Historical Society. Many of my writer friends have told me that every good writer has to begin their talk with a story about themselves and about the writing of the book. So, I think one of the things that I experienced that I found particularly perplexing I wanted to share with you, and it was about two weeks before my book was due to go off to the printer. I was in big trouble. While preparing it for publication, I was also learning how to use my computer software and formatting and stylization.

I couldn't get the pagination correct, and I was frantically searching the program book to find out exactly what I should be doing, and the guidebook makes the assumption that one that is using that guidebook has already had some experience with the computer, so certain basic steps are overlooked. Well, I followed it to the letter to the best of my ability and got into deeper trouble, and after about a week of trying to extricate myself from that, I gave in, and I called the emergency helpline that was listed.

My call was answered by a person that sounded like a male teenager, who listened to my problem and with weary patience, questioned my process, and when I explained what I had done and told him that I had followed the book to the letter, he firmly told me it was totally wrong and to follow his instructions. Well, when I asked him, "how is it possible that it was wrong, this is what the book says, I'm doing exactly what they said," in a tone of voice reserved undoubtedly only for female middle-aged computer novices, he said to me, "now Jacqueline, you listen to me, you throw the book away. You listen to me, don't you pay any attention to it, destroy it. Do you understand me? Do exactly what I'm saying to you. Do you understand?" I meekly said "yes, I do," and told him that I would follow his advice to the letter. He, of course, knew better than I. Well, by the time I finished making the changes, I was totally exhausted, and decided it was enough for one day and would start the next using his format.

So, as I began doing only what he told me to do, I found myself again in deep trouble. Yes, that's right. He gave me wrong advice. So, I spent another week of telephone conversations before the mess was corrected, but I was able to meet my deadline. So, the moral of it is that we must all continue to learn to trust ourselves to get us to the frontier, be it Ohio or the land of computers.

But on a serious note, I told my writer friends that there certainly was really nothing funny about this book; there was certainly nothing funny about her experiences; and that the rarity of finding such a collection of letters that span a twenty-year period in a woman's life from her arrival in Ohio to her death in Ohio has been confirmed by several historians with whom I have been in contact.

The letters are a wonderful description of life on the frontier, its sadness and its tribulations, and is the story of Mary Phillips Lott, her husband Henry, and Mary's brother Thomas. And since Mary's grave is unknown, I feel that my book marks Mary's memory and place in history. It also shows what is common among women from the period, and that is that documentation of Mary's life on Earth, with the exception of these letters, is just about non-existent.

The difficulty in researching women's lives and the scarcity of locating records tells the common story of women's history, and that is why it really is lacking in depth. That is why a book such as this is so important to let people know exactly what women experienced. So, it was necessary, it was absolutely necessary, to get this book published so that one woman's history could be preserved.

The quote from Mary's letters that I use in the front of the book says, "once more I lift my pen to let you know that through the mercy of Him that never sleeps nor slumbers, we are all alive and in common health."

She expresses this fact throughout her letters, her gratitude to be in common health, and the faith that sustained her, and what I'd like to share with you this evening are some of the events mentioned in the letters by Mary, and I will relate them to some of the circumstances of women as well as the shared views of frontier women of that period, 1826 to 1846.

I will begin by telling you a little of the background of Mary and John, since I'm sure there are many of you that are not familiar with their story. John Phillips, Deacon John Phillips, was born in 1752, and he is my Revolutionary War grandfather. Mary, born about 1782; they were brother and sister by the same father Francis Phillips, but probably by different mothers. It is presumed that John's mother Demis Aylesworth died when John was about 14 years old since he is mentioned in his grandfather Aylesworth's will, but his mother is not.

And because of the disparate differences in the sibling's ages, it's believed that Francis, John's father who was born in West Greenwich Rhode Island in 1720, was married twice and probably three times. There is also a Bible record that exists showing four other sons. Zacchaeus and Francis, whom I believe I located in New York State as late as 1825, 1830; a brother Thomas, who apparently went with Mary Lott to Ohio, first in New York State; and then Cornwell, the youngest, who I also found on a New York State census with wife and children, and who probably died somewhere between 1843 and 1846 since one letter from Mary is written to his wife, which indicates that by this point, she was alone in Pennsylvania.

John was thirty years old when Mary was born, and Mary's father was 62 years old. This is quite common for the period. Today this is considered very unusual but was not during that period. Also common was the fact of women giving birth into their 40s and well into their 50s.

Francis Phillips, John's father, was a member of the Connecticut Land Company; it was a company that was formed to purchase land in Pennsylvania. I have located Francis Phillips as early as 1771 in Pennsylvania when the Wyoming Valley was called the Westmoreland County of the State of Connecticut.

It would be many years of bitter conflict between the Yankees and William Penn's people before ownership of all of the land in this region could be documented and proven. John Phillips' claims were well-documented, and his land ownership was approved by about 1791. It was a long time that they had to wait for this because he was here during the revolution and had land then, so you can see it was many years before that took place. However, I found no further proof of claims by Francis Phillips.

John and Mary were separated, a fact that's referred to often in her letters, probably after the death of their father Francis somewhere between 1788 and 1791 that is documented by land records that referred to him as being "now deceased." His son John served from three states during the Revolutionary War, New York, Vermont, and Pennsylvania, and he did go on to become what was considered a very wealthy landowner and owned thousands of acres in the region between Scranton and Wilkes-Barre.

He was a deacon in the First Baptist Church, and he gave very generous gifts of land to his children and to his grandchildren. Old Deacon John lived to the age of 94 years and eight months. He was married three times, the third time at the age of 90 years old. He had six children, eighty-eight grandchildren, and uncounted great-grandchildren at his death in 1846.

That's why I know I'm related to everybody in this area after all those grandchildren. There are many families in the area who are related to John, including the Millers, the Tripps, the Wilsons, the Russells, the Wilcoxes, the Hewitts, it goes on and on. I'm descended through the Miller line. His daughter Susannah Phillips married Samuel Miller, so this is how the Millers started. My father died two years ago at the age of 86, and his father lived until almost 91, so there is the longevity which exists there.

Well, when I came to Scranton to explore the Miller-Phillips line, this was a very interesting treasure hunt, and the Historical Society is absolutely wonderful and a joy to come to and deal with. I do feel we have friends here.

I had some correspondence with Mary Ann about the Phillips line, and she would always tell me about the collection of Hildah Phillips Brown. I had no idea what I was going to find until my husband and I arrived in Scranton and set upon the table in the back room were cartons and cartons filled to overflowing with papers from the collection of Hildah Philips Brown. This woman was extraordinary. She started her search many, many years ago over a twenty-five-to-thirty-year period right up until the time of her death in about 1962. Hildah Phillips Brown was a very conservative lady in terms of saving things. Her notes were kept on envelopes, old shopping lists, backs of bills. I mean, it was amazing to go through this.

Well, there in the bottom of this box were these letters, and Mary Ann had also mentioned that to me at one point, and I really had no concept of what this was going to be, and at the bottom of this box was a collection of letters copied from the originals. We do not know where the originals exist, but Hildah had the originals by 1968. They are referred to in an article written by the Abington Journal.

What Hildah had done was she had painstakingly hand-copied each and every one of these letters on long pieces of shelf paper to use as a tool to further her investigation of the genealogy of the Phillips and the Miller line. There were just reams and reams and reams of paper, all of these letters just kind of one after another, and she had copied them the way Mary Lott had written them. No punctuation, no capitalizations, misspellings, and so forth. So, she had used them as a working guide in doing her search.

Through clues in her letters, I tracked Mary Lott and her husband Henry Lott to Genesee County, New York, in an area, interestingly enough, not far from my hometown of Buffalo. I had no idea, of course, when I lived in Buffalo that she even existed, and I found it interesting and very serendipitous that she had actually lived just a few miles from where I was raised.

Susan [Poulson] talked about John Smith being located in that region, and I have wondered whether there might have been some connection. I wondered, were they followers of, excuse me, Joseph Smith, were they followers of his? Were they possibly early followers of the Mormon Church? There's nothing in the letters that refer to that. Maybe it was just an interesting circumstance, but the paths seem to cross one another, however, I was not able to locate any documents in the state of New York that confirmed that Henry and Mary Lott lived there.

Part of the Lott family remained in Wyoming County, Pennsylvania, while others already had moved to Delaware County, Ohio, with Henry's father Zephaniah Lott. Zephaniah was a Revolutionary War veteran who went to Ohio, as did many Pennsylvanians, to obtain land available to veterans of the Revolutionary War. So, there's many Pennsylvania families there. Many towns have names the same as towns in this area, Kingston and so forth. There's a wide number of them.

So, I did find several documents on file in Delaware County, Ohio, to show their residence. However, it is only in the letters that the full story is told of their existence. Her letters begin upon their arrival in Ohio, in which she describes a frontier existence no different from that of the men in her life. She was equal partner in the hardships and drudgeries of everyday activities, and often was expected to go far beyond what we may think of as her fair share of the load.

But she did appear to be a true partner of her husband Henry, and in many examples in her letters, she appears to be the decision maker. This is a circumstance shared by many frontier women. Necessity provided the need for women to be self-sustaining and independent. This was a very important first for women.

Her first letter is dated October 8th, 1826, and by the way, we do know that letters are missing; there are gaps in the dates. So, I often would wonder what are in those letters that I don't have that would fill in these gaps, and we may never know.

But fortunately, we do have the first letter dated October 8th, 1826, and Mary gives many details in that letter, which really doesn't tell the whole story of her journey. She says, "We came from Buffalo [New York] to Portland [Ohio] on the steamboat; had good luck, was two days and two nights on water, but we had a very tedious journey from there in consequence of rain and new roads. We found it about 100 miles."

The fact of the matter was that life's rules of conduct were quite controlled in those days, particularly for women, and what she does not make reference to is that in the 1820s, new transportation modes such as steamboats caused new expectations of behavior.

There were various attempts to segregate the sexes, both on board these steamships and in waiting rooms. While traveling on a steamboat, an English woman writer of the period describes the men's cabin on the boat as the more desirable and says, "their exclusive right to it is somewhat uncourteously insisted upon." She also described the fact that husbands and wives were separated throughout the entire journey and could only be together at mealtimes. We can assume that Mary, her husband, and brother had to comply with these rules as well.

She goes on to describe their difficult Ohio beginnings by saying quite simply, "we have bought 50 acres of entirely new land joining Leonard's (Henry's brother)." "Got two log rooms raised, the bigness of our old rooms in Stafford," a town in Genesee County, New York.

However, in another letter, Mary refers to financial difficulties when she says, "there was $54.00 behind on our place we did not get. I think, in consequence of not taking my advice. The man came for the deed. I told [Henry] not to give it up till he got the money, but [the man] said he should have it next day. We waited two weeks, could not get it—had to come away suing the note and leaving the business with Anson Williams."

Women were normally excluded from business decisions, but it is obvious that Mary had a better sense for business arrangements than Henry because, at today's value, that $54 they were owed was worth at least $10,000.

Mary was probably born about 1782 in the Wyoming Valley in Pennsylvania while it was also the frontier to where her father Francis had emigrated from Rhode Island. When he died, as I said earlier, we know it was no later than 1791, and probably more like 1788. English and Colonial law still influenced life of the period, so after a husband's death, a widow was not allowed to be guardian to her own children after they reached a certain age if ownership of property was involved. By law, the mother was not allowed to oversee it.

Also, the death of a husband often necessitated selling the homestead to pay off his debts, another obligation required by law. A mother might then be forced to send children to other families as bond servants if she could not afford to keep them. In these instances, a guardian would be appointed by the court or could also be selected by the child, and in Mary's case, there is a record in the probate records of Luzerne County, Pennsylvania in about 1796 in which she was described as a minor over the age of 14.

I wanted to also refer to the fact that at that period of time, particularly going on into an unknown frontier, sickness and health problems certainly overpowered and predominated family life. Necessity forced the women to not only be the caretakers, but also to overlook their own needs and illnesses, and Mary makes reference to that in her letters when she says in a letter of February 1827, "my health continued much the same it was when I wrote you a few days after we moved when I was taken very poorly and have been so ever since. I have every complaint any woman can have of my age besides a broken constitution, yet I have not been entirely confined. But I have had to work every moment I could for something to live on as our money was gone last fall."

And another reference again is to the fact that, "We are at present all in common health. I have been very unwell with a disorder that has prevailed in this neighborhood. 'Twas something like a very bad cold, but I am now better. The widow Bartley died with it about five weeks ago. I think she might have lived had she have had care and things for her comfort in the first of her sickness, but help was afforded too late. I was sick at the time, and I did not get there quite a week before she died. But she died in the triumphs of a living faith and fondly committed her four little children in the hands of the Lord, saying she knew He would take better care of them than she could."

It's not known where Mary spent her early years, but when discussing mutual family friends in a letter, Mary relates, "Abraham says the tender tie of friendship felt for me in childhood when I was separated from all relatives are yet the same, and although we have been separated so many years, yet he believes with you and me that time or distance can never [break] those tender ties of friendship."

Her unhappy childhood is very obvious throughout her writings when Mary refers to herself as a "child of sorrow." It is possible that Mary's mother remarried and as was common, children may also have been sent to other family members or friends to take care of. Certainly, separations were very common in that period.

She says in the same letter, "often of late with most solemn reflections, I recall my past life from my childhood till the present moment; the many separations of dear friends, some by death and particular the moment, my bosom heaves forth the big sigh, while tears gives vent to my almost bursting heart, but ere, I am aware Jesus appears and fills my soul with glory and seems to say 'I am still thy friend though thorns and briars has always marked your ways.'"

Mary's strong religious faith is apparent certainly throughout her letters. It's a faith that is verbalized in many other diaries and letters of frontier women, and it's interesting to note that after the American Revolution, church attendance decreased due to the new separation of church and state. With exceptions, it remained in decline throughout the country.

However, during the first quarter of the 19th Century, the religious revival churches made a concerted effort to widen membership and finding that males were less influenced in daily life by religion than females, ministers recognized that faith was of immediate concern to women. Some scholars suggest that women, although accepting of men as church leaders, also quickly learned that there were few places outside the home where autonomy was allowed and accepted other than the church.

Therefore, religion came to be accepted by the men as women's realm. To the women on the frontier, maintaining Protestantism was one of their greatest challenges. It satisfied their spiritual needs certainly as well and explains their daily lives. All things were the will of God.

Evangelical revivals gave women the opportunity to take control of their own lives and to be given essential roles. Participation in camp meetings and revivals were often referred to as the feminization of religion and they gave women the opportunity to become leaders and charismatic figures in their own right. But the most important aspect for women was the socialization and feelings of security that they provided through their relationships with other women.

Mary's interest in involvement with religion is expressed in one of her letters when she says, "the inhabitants appear very friendly, and meetings are handy of almost all kinds, though no particular revivals of religion at present."

In another letter, she says, "I have stayed home from meeting to let you know we are all in common health." In still another, she says, "it is almost meeting time and I must omit some things I would have wrote, for I should have wrote finer had I not been in such haste."

Historians say that the Presbyterian religion was among the best organized in Ohio. Mary makes reference to that when she says, "The Presbyterians have had a protracted meeting and it lasted almost two weeks, night and day. There was near forty moved forward and about twenty professed to obtain a hope in Jesus. May they ever stand fast in that liberty where with Christ has made them free." In the 1830s, the issue of the abolition of slavery became a natural outgrowth of women's domestic and religious life and was a precursor to women's suffrage. Mary's brother John apparently had strong opinions regarding this matter, as did Mary, since in a letter dated 1838, Mary says, "We return you many thanks for your papers. We think them very good and their opinion on slavery exactly with my mind, for ever since I come to years of understanding, I believe slavery a great evil and an abomination in the eyes of our Heavenly Father, and for such enmity to be suffered in a nation that has been so cried up for a land of liberty. And I do believe if something is not done soon to alleviate the sufferings of the poor slaves, that the Lord will deliver them as he did the children of Israel some way or another, and as a nation we shall be scourged, for the beautiful true liberty [will] no more flourish, for the limbs are already loped and the leaves are withering."

I find that particularly beautiful, that paragraph.

Communication with family and other women friends was very important, and the commonality of Mary's pleas for family to move to the frontier is seen in other examples of women's frontier writings. And if they couldn't get relatives to move to the frontier, then they were always making plans to go visit the family back at the old family home, but often these plans were not carried off.

Concerns about feminine appearance and proper clothing are also very prominent among these plans to visit home, and Mary shares her worries when she says, "I shall try very hard to come, if we all have our health and can possibly get a little spending money and a few clothes…that I think you will not be ashamed of me."

And if family or friends couldn't come or visits couldn't be made back home, then women had faith that relatives and friends would come together in Heaven. This belief sustained them, as it did Mary, and when after a disappointment of not being able to make a trip to Pennsylvania, she says, "my determination is to see you, should the Lord spare our lives and health. And my prayer is that Jesus may be your best and dearest friend and support the tottering frames till we meet again in this life, but if not here, I fully believe we shall in Heaven when this short voyage of life shall end."

I wanted to read another letter in the book that expresses the tragedy of death and illness and the joy of rebirth, all in one point:

"Once more I sit down to let you know we are alive and in common health, through the goodness of our heavenly Father, though with sorrowful heart, I have to inform you that our dear sister Hannah has been called to follow her daughter Lucena to the silent grave from whence no traveler ere returned. She had not yet seen eighteen years and had been married almost three years. She had a baby last September, but it died at six weeks old. She left no family but her husband. She was like the fair flower that fades before noon. The first cause of her illness was the chill and fever; a year last winter, they moved out to the Sandusky Plains. She was taken very sick two years ago but got better so her father brought her home in one room before she was confined where she lived and died."

She goes on to talk about her family and the children left behind. Mary visited her in the beginning of her illness, and said, "I talked with her and gained full satisfaction the last she talked in connection, though she spoke sentences till almost the last breath. She called her father and mother and brothers and sisters to the bed and her other friends and took them by the hand, talked to them one by one, giving them some token of her affection and saying, 'farewell, remember dying Lucena, meet me in Heaven.'"

So, these are the common sounds of the letters going from tragedy to happy events. The poignancy of the life of frontier women is described by another writer who said that "clinging to a few treasured heirlooms as reminders of a kinder life, they accompanied their husbands, suffering the most disparate physical hardships as well as the desolating sense of loneliness."

Mary's loneliness and despair becomes more apparent as the years pass and, at the end, she is without family members. After Mary's husband Henry died, as was the custom, an inventory of possessions was taken and included, along with the description of farm implements and a short list of household items: Mary's two spinning wheels, her loom, two bibles, six other books and, incongruously, one red fan.

A memento from a happier time and place perhaps, it evokes a vision of a young woman filled with hopes and dreams moving forward into the future. And although as we read her story, her trials and tribulations may fill us with a sad recognition, her life of hardship was shared by many women who were carving a path in the wilderness for us to follow.

Mary Lott died in 1846 a few months after the death of her brother John, and I believe she died when she received the news of John's death. She, throughout her letters, certainly refers to her fear that soon she will hear that he has died.

But we should not think of Mary as a tragic symbol. Rather, she was a woman of strength, courage, and faith, and her life should be considered a proud tribute to all the women who went before and came after clutching and cherishing their own red fans.

My Cousin, Elizabeth Cady Stanton

United Nations 50th Anniversary Luncheon
Sponsored by the National Council of Women
New York, March 31, 1995

Madame President, Fellow Board Members, Distinguished Guests, you have honored me greatly with your invitation to address you today. It is with a great feeling of pride and a personal sense of history that I appear before you.

Many outstanding women have preceded me with words that changed the lives of women around the world. Many went on to become recognized figures in all areas of society.

It is a humbling experience to be included in that formidable group of sisters who form a unique sorority by virtue of their appearance before this great body, The National Council of Women.

It is equally humbling to speak to you in this great building, The United Nations. Had she lived in our time, it is certain that Elizabeth Cady Stanton, my distinguished relative and co-founder of The International Council of Women and The National Council of Women, would have made herself heard before the UN's illustrious assemblage, as she did before many government bodies.

During this day of celebration and recognition of the 50th anniversary of the United Nations, as well as the 108th anniversary of the International Council of Women and the National Council of Women, it is fitting that we remember Elizabeth Cady Stanton.

Elizabeth Cady Stanton, her husband Henry Brewster Stanton, and I are descended from our common ancestor Thomas Stanton, who was married to Katherine

Washington, a cousin to George Washington. Their grandson Thomas Stanton and his wife Anna Lord had several children, including Hannah, Joseph, and John.

It is through these three siblings that we are related. Elizabeth through Hannah, Henry through Joseph, and I through John. Elizabeth and Henry were fifth cousins, and I am a cousin, tenth generation, to both.

Elizabeth Cady was born in 1815 in Johnstown, N.Y. On her mother's side, she was descended from the oldest and wealthiest families of the high society classes of New York, including the Beekmans, Schuylers, Van Rensselaers, Ten Broecks, and Livingstons, large landowners with huge estates on the Hudson who were leaders in the business, social, and political life of New York.

Elizabeth was also influenced by the liberal and reformist family of her noted abolitionist cousin, Gerrit Smith, of Peterboro, N. Y. There is no question that relationships opened many doors for Cady Stanton, as she like to be called, as she pursued her destiny.

Known as "the foremost American woman intellectual of her generation," Cady Stanton was involved in a search for "...underlying principles of human and social behavior."

A feminist, reformer, public figure, and self-described radical, she never wrote a lengthy analytical work. To influence opinion toward women she turned to oratory and journalism.

Her original plan for an international women's organization had been to focus on suffrage issues. However, the agenda for the first meeting was broadened to include a wider range of topics, both political and social. Stanton, however, refused to authorize an invitation to women who were opposed to women's suffrage.

To celebrate the fortieth anniversary of the Seneca Falls convention, The International Council of Women opened in Washington, D.C. on March 25, 1888, and lasted for one week to April 1, 1888.

Over eighty speakers were heard as fifty-three organizations and forty-nine delegates from England, France, Ireland, Norway, Finland, India, Canada, and the United States met.

"Literary Clubs, Art Unions, Temperance Unions, Labor Leagues, Missionary, Peace and Moral Purity Societies, Charitable, Professional, Educational and Industrial Associations [were] "thus offered equal opportunity with Suffrage Societies to be represented in what should be the ablest and most imposing body of women ever assembled."

President and Mrs. Grover Cleveland welcomed the delegates with a reception. Reverend Anna Shaw, an associate of Frances Willard, preached the Sunday Sermon at the grand opera house. Soft music played in the large auditorium and evergreens and flowers filled the platform. A portrait of Lucretia Mott was hung above, surrounded by smilax and lilies of the valley.

Susan B. Anthony opened the first session, welcoming the huge throng and saying, "I have the pleasure of introducing to you this morning the woman who not only joined with Lucretia Mott in calling the first convention, but who for the greater part of twenty years has been president of the National Woman's Suffrage Association, Mrs. Elizabeth Cady Stanton."

Cady Stanton was seventy-three years old, plump, matronly, and with white hair arranged in her signatory mass of curls when she appeared at the International

Council meeting. She had been involved with women's reform work for over forty-eight years.

As she moved forward on the stage, the body of delegates rose as one with great applause and waved their white handkerchiefs. The predominant theme at the convention was the solidarity of women and their universal sisterhood. The "representative women" included in the council had been defined in terms broader than any other women's congress of the time.

Reflecting the diversity of women, the council "...impress[ed] the important lesson that the position of the women anywhere affects their position everywhere."

In her opening speech, Cady Stanton addressed the delegates by saying, "in welcoming representatives from other lands here today, we do not feel that you are strangers and foreigners, for the women of all nationalities, in the artificial distinctions of sex, have a universal sense of injustice that forms a common bond of union between them."

She emphasized women's similarities when she said it is "...through suffering...that women share experience regardless of class, [whether]...housed in golden cages with every want supplied, or wandering in the dreary deserts of life, friendless and forsaken..."

She went on to say, "the true woman is as yet a dream of the future. A just government, a humane religion, a pure social life awaits her coming. Then and not till then, will the golden age of peace and prosperity be ours..."

Before the conference closed, the National Council of Women was established to bring together all women's organizations in a partnership of strength. It became the first multi-reform national women's organization founded in the United States. Its initial goals included equal pay for women, availability to education both

212

professional and industrial, and a single standard of morals for both men and women.

Although she lived a life of comfort, Cady Stanton rejected the wealthy woman's privileged relationships of status, class, background, and heritage to spend a lifetime working toward a new relationship and definition of power.

In her closing statement at the council, she asked, "Where can we look for the new power whereby the race [of humankind] can be lifted up?" She answered by declaring that the future lay in women's hands.

The international sisterhood in which she believed and the movement toward world understanding of women's issues has, over time, manifested itself in the continuation of The International and National Councils of Women, and the United Nation's fifty years of effort.

Although we have not finished the work that she and her friends started, we say thank you Cady Stanton for helping to pave the way for the women of the world.

Research for this presentation is from the following:

Anthony, Susan B., and Ida Harper. *History of Woman Suffrage;* Volume 4, Rochester; Susan B. Anthony; 1903.

Banner, Lois W. *Elizabeth Cady Stanton; A Radical for Women's Rights.* Boston; Little & Brown, 1980.

Barry, Kathleen. *Susan B. Anthony: A Biography.* New York & London; New York University Press.1988.

DuBois, Ellen C. *Elizabeth Cady Stanton, Susan B. Anthony; Correspondence, Writings, Speeches.* New York: Shocken Books, 1981.

Genealogical Research; New England Historical Society. Boston, Massachusetts.

Griffith, Elisabeth. *In Her Own Right; The Life of Elizabeth Cady Stanton.* New York: Oxford University Press, 1984.

International Council of Women Papers, Founding Convention. Washington D.C.

UN Under Secretary Joseph Verner Reed & Jacqueline Bachar

My Cousin, Elizabeth Cady Stanton (NCW)

Elizabeth Cady Stanton Birthday Celebration,
Stanton Foundation, Women's Rights Historical Park,
Seneca Falls, New York, November 12, 1995

Madam President, Board members of the Stanton Foundation, ladies and gentlemen, it is a great pleasure to be here in Seneca Falls and a special privilege to attend the birthday celebration of Elizabeth Cady Stanton.

It is fitting that the dedication of a special tribute to the 75th anniversary of the passage of the 19th amendment should take place on this day. It's an auspicious time to be on the East coast. My husband Paul and I are ex-New York Staters now living in the Los Angeles area. We came here so that I could continue my research for a biography of Elizabeth Cady Stanton.

We have visited her home in Tenafly, met with her great-granddaughter Barney-Jenkins and her daughter Coline, visited the Seneca Falls Historical Society and, of course, the Stanton home here in Seneca Falls.

This year has seen another important event acknowledged—the 50th anniversary of the United Nations. 1995 is also the 107th anniversary of the National Council of Women, an organization founded by Elizabeth Cady Stanton, Susan B. Anthony, and others.

Stanton and her colleagues recognized the importance of anniversaries. They selected the 40th anniversary of the first women's convention held here in Seneca Falls to convene the *First International Council of Women* in Washington, D.C. There the National Council of Women was also formed, now making it the oldest existing woman's coalition volunteer organization in the country.

The National Council of Women has consultative status as a Non-Governmental Organization with the United Nations. Therefore, it was fitting that a joint celebration was held there this past March. I was asked to speak to the august body about my distinguished relative, Elizabeth Cady Stanton.

Stanton made her appearance through me and through her words which I presented to the Deputy Secretary-General of the United Nations, the Ambassadors to the United Nations, and the board members and guests of the National Council of Women.

The words that I used to describe my feelings appearing in that great setting before those outstanding men and women were equal to my feelings of being here today in another great and special building that is dedicated to the outstanding women and events of this country.

Elizabeth Cady Stanton unites us here today with those of the past and future on this, her birthday. I'd like to share with you the story told at the United Nations, where many people heard of her for the first time. Many of the details are already known to most of you here, but it is fitting that we review them as a remembrance and a celebration of her life.

But first, let me tell you how we are related. Elizabeth Cady, her husband Henry Brewster Stanton, and I are descended from our common ancestor, Thomas Stanton, who was married to Katherine Washington, a cousin to George Washington. Their grandson Thomas Stanton was a founder of Stonington, Connecticut.

He and his wife Anna Lord had several children, including Hannah, Joseph, and John. It is through these three siblings that we are related. Elizabeth through Hannah, Henry through Joseph, and I through John.

Elizabeth and Henry were fifth cousins, a fact I discovered in research through the New England Historical and Genealogical Society in Boston. I am a cousin, tenth generation, to both, and although a distant relative, it is a connection of which I am most proud.

Elizabeth and I are related to Presidents Herbert Hoover and Gerald Ford. She is also kinswoman to Presidents Van Buren and Theodore Roosevelt. She was second cousin to diplomat Robert Livingston and Mrs. Alexander Hamilton. She was also of royal descent through her mother's family, the Livingstons.

Through his Brewster line, Henry Stanton is related to the Rockefellers and the Princess of Wales, and was descended from the French King Hugh Capet, from whom all French Kings and other Royals are descended.

Therefore, the blood of many nations and their leaders flows through our veins. All these relationships were discovered after I became involved with the International Council of Women while I was living in Belgium, and later with the National Council of Women.

It is humbling to wonder about the serendipitous nature of that. One must also wonder about the events in an individual's life that leads to a certain path. There is no question that relationships opened many doors for Cady Stanton, as she like to be called, as she pursued her destiny.

She is with me today as she was at the United Nations. She unites us through family ties as she unites each of us sitting here, and those individuals of the past and future through her great work for us as women. During this day of celebration and recognition of her birthday, the 50th anniversary of the United Nations, as well as the 107th anniversary of the International Council of Women and the National Council of Women, it is fitting that we remember Elizabeth Cady Stanton.

Elizabeth Cady was born in 1815, in Johnstown, N.Y. On her mother's side, she was descended from the oldest and wealthiest families, high society classes of New York, including the Beekmans, Schuylers, Van Rensselaers, Ten Broecks, and the Livingstons, landowners with huge estates on the Hudson and leaders in New York's business, social, and political worlds. Despite these relations, Elizabeth was also influenced by the liberal and reformist family of her noted abolitionist cousin, Gerrit Smith, of Peterboro, New York.

It was there that she met Henry Stanton, a renowned anti-slavery speaker ten years older than she. He had no money of his own and no prospects of inheritance, but Elizabeth was taken with him and against the disapproval of her parents married him a month later. An aspect of the hurried nature of this pertained to his promise to take her to the World Anti-Slavery Convention in London.

They were married in Johnstown, N.Y., where Elizabeth Cady insisted on retaining her own name and adding her husband's name to it. She would always refer to herself as Cady Stanton. She also requested the word "obey" be eliminated from the marriage ceremony. They honeymooned in London, where she met Lucretia Mott, another founder of the National Council of Women.

Elizabeth's grandfather James Cady was in the Revolutionary War and was a member of the New York State Assembly and of the Board of Regents of the State University. Elizabeth Cady's father, Daniel Cady, was the son of a farmer. Daniel worked as a blacksmith and went on to study law and become a lawyer.

His reputation as an expert on land law was outstanding, which in 1801 enabled him to marry the wealthy Margaret Livingston. Daniel went on to serve in the New York State Assembly for several terms and served one term in the House of Representatives. In 1847, he became a justice of the New York Supreme Court.

Elizabeth Cady Stanton, known as "the foremost American woman intellectual of her generation," was involved in a search for "underlying principles of human and social behavior" and during her lifetime, a self-described radical. She became an anti-slavery advocate when the Civil War began, and with other women leaders of the time found her way from the abolitionist movement to subsequent women's issues. A "new woman," reformer and public figure, she never wrote a lengthy analytical work. To influence opinion toward women she turned to oratory and journalism.

Elizabeth had planned on a visit to England and France to have an international conference for many years. Her original plan for an international women's organization had been to focus on suffrage issues. However, in 1888, when it became a reality, the agenda for the first meeting now included a broader range of women's issues, political and social.

To celebrate the fortieth anniversary of the Seneca Falls convention, The International Council of Women was held in Washington, D.C. from March 25, 1888, until April 1, 1888. Fifty-three organizations and forty-nine delegates from England, France, Ireland, Norway, Finland, India, Canada, and the United States met, during which time over eighty speakers were heard.

"Literary Clubs, Art Unions, Temperance Unions, Labor Leagues, Missionary, Peace and Moral Purity

Societies, Charitable, Professional, Educational and Industrial Associations [are] thus offered equal opportunity with Suffrage Societies to be represented in what should be the ablest and most imposing body of women ever assembled."

Mailings sent to potential participants discussed practical matters such as railroad costs, hotels and boarding houses and their rates and cost of tickets to The International Council. The Riggs House reduced their daily rate to $3.00 and other hotels to $2.50 and $2.00. Daily meals ran from $4.00 to $7.00 per week. Tickets to the council were from 25 cents for a single admission to $4.00 for the entire session with reserved seating. Susan B. Anthony reported that The National Woman Suffrage Association would issue daily, during the Council, the *"Woman's Tribune.* containing a full report of the proceedings."

The report described the Saturday reception at the Riggs House for the officers and delegates of the Council. The flag-filled dining room and other public rooms, although crowded, were "gratifying to the participants" who remained until midnight.

President and Mrs. Grover Cleveland welcomed the delegates with a reception. Reverend Anna Shaw, an associate of Frances Willard, preached the Sunday sermon at the grand-opera house. In the large auditorium soft music played, and evergreens and flowers filled the platform. A portrait of Lucretia Mott hung above, surrounded by smilax and lilies of the valley.

On Monday, March 26, the Council began with "The Promised Land" by Elizabeth Boynton Harbert, the opening stanza as follows;

"Our weary years of wandering o'er,
We greet with joy this radiant shore;
The promised land of liberty.
The dawn of freedom's morn we see,
O, promised land, we enter in,
With "Peace on earth, good-will to men,"
The "Golden Age" now comes again,
As breaketh every bond and chain;
While every race and sect and clime
Shall equal-share in this glad time."

Susan B. Anthony, Elizabeth's longtime friend, announced the formal opening of the Council, welcoming the huge throng by saying, "I have the pleasure of introducing to you this morning the woman who not only joined with Lucretia Mott in calling the first convention, but who for the greater part of twenty years has been president of the National Woman's Suffrage Association—Mrs. Elizabeth Cady Stanton."

Mrs. Stanton was seventy-three years old, plump, matronly, with white hair arranged in her signatory mass of curls when she appeared at the International Council meeting. As she moved forward on the stage, the body of delegates rose as one with great applause and waved their white handkerchiefs. The predominant theme at the convention was solidarity of women and their universal sisterhood.

The "representative women" included in the council had been defined in much broader terms than any other women's congress of the time. Reflecting the diversity of women, the council "impress[ed] the important lesson that the position of the women anywhere affects their position everywhere."

In her opening speech, "Cady Stanton addressed the delegates by saying; "in welcoming representatives from other lands here today, we do not feel that you are strangers and foreigners, for the women of all nationalities, in the artificial distinctions of sex, have a universal sense of injustice that forms a common bond of union between them."

She emphasized women's similarities when she said it is "through suffering" that women share experience regardless of class, [whether] "housed in golden cages with every want supplied, or wandering in the dreary deserts of life, friendless and forsaken..." She went on to say that "the true woman is as yet a dream of the future. A just government, a humane religion, a pure social life awaits her coming. Then and not till then, will the golden age of peace and prosperity be ours..."

Each session included up-lifting anthems and hymns such as "The New America," "New Columbia," and "The Equal-Rights Banner" sung to the tune of the Star-spangled Banner. The morning and evening sessions were divided into various themes, such as Temperance, Industries, Professions, and Legal and Political Conditions.

They featured speakers representing groups and organizations working within each area. Representative of these were Clara Barton, President of the American Red Cross, Julia Ward Howe, President of the Association of the Advancement of Women, and Amelia S. Quinton, President of the Women's National Indian Association.

On the final weekend, the Conference of the Pioneers included speakers such as Frederick Douglas, Susan B. Anthony, Lucy Stone, Antoinette Brown Blackwell, and of course, Elizabeth Cady Stanton, who on Sunday gave the closing remarks.

Before the conference closed, the National Council of Women was established to bring together all women's organizations in a partnership of strength. It became the first multi-reform national women's organization founded in the United States. Its initial goals included equal pay for women, availability to education both professional and industrial, and a single standard of morals for both men and women.

Although she lived a life of comfort, Cady Stanton rejected the wealthy woman's privileged relationships of status, class, background, and heritage to spend a lifetime working toward a new relationship and definition of power. In her closing statement, she asked, "where can we look for the new power whereby the race [of humankind] can be lifted up?" She answered by declaring that in women's hands lay the future.

The international sisterhood that she believed in and the movement toward world understanding of women's issues has manifested itself over time through the continuation of The International and National Councils of Women, and the United Nation's fifty years of effort. Although we have not finished the work that she and her friends started, I say thank you cousin Cady Stanton, for helping to pave the way for the women of the world.

Elizabeth Cady Stanton & Mary Lott (2014)

National Society Daughters of the American Revolution,
Cahuilla Chapter, March 17, 2014

Good afternoon, Regent Hardy, Board Members, Fellow Daughters, and Guests. Thank you for the opportunity to talk to you today about women in history. I will begin with my distinguished distant cousin and women's rights advocate Elizbeth Cady Stanton, who in her prime was the most famous woman in America.

I will then introduce you to Mary Lott, my great, great, great aunt, and sister of my Revolutionary War ancestor John Phillips, born around 1782 into a unique family of revolutionaries, men of the church and later, wealthy landowners.

Mary spent her remaining life in great difficulty in what was then the frontier, torn from her family. Her sad separation is told in my book of Mary Lott's letters, *Life on the Ohio Frontier: A Collection of Letters from Mary Lott to Deacon John Phillips 1826-1846*. I have brought copies here today for your perusal.

Cady Stanton, as she liked to be called, was about eleven when at the time of Mary Lott's first letters and was in her thirties at the time of the last. Mary left Genesee County, New York to make the difficult journey from Buffalo via Lake Erie on a steamboat to Portland, Ohio, and from there traveled a hundred miles overland to her home in the wilderness. Elizabeth Cady would be influenced by the preachers of her time in Genesee County. It was women like Mary who Elizabeth Cady fought for later in life.

Cady Stanton, Mary, and I are bonded by the blood of mutual ancestors and united through family ties. These two women personify the many women who paved the way in the past through their work and struggles for all women, uniting all of us sitting here today and eventually those of the future yet to be born. It is fitting that we remember them during Women's History Month.

My late husband Paul and I lived in Brussels, Belgium for four years. He was Director of Europe for the Space & Communications Satellite Program with Hughes Aircraft. While we were there, I worked for the President of the International Council of Women. When we returned to the states, I became a member of the National Council of Women, later serving on its national board. It was later when I continued my family genealogy work that I learned I was related to Cady Stanton, a co-founder of the International Council of Women, and later the National Council. How serendipitous is that?

Who was my distant cousin Elizabeth Cady Stanton? I would guess that many, if not most of you in this room know her name. Some who have studied women's history know of her accomplishments and failures, but the average person hasn't got a clue.

For example, in 1995, I was privileged to speak at the 50th anniversary of the United Nations, where we also celebrated the 107th anniversary of the International and National Council of Women. I spoke about Cady Stanton. After I spoke, United Nations Under Secretary General Joseph Verner Reed asked if I would give him a copy of my speech. He said he didn't know this fascinating woman, was a friend of documentary filmmaker Ken Burns, and that he would like to tell him about her.

I gave him a copy of my speech and forgot about it until many years later when a documentary by Ken Burns about Elizabeth Cady Stanton was on PBS. While I enjoyed it, my name didn't appear anywhere in the credits, and I wondered if my speech had played a small role in its making. It's a fun story to ponder. ***

By the time Elizabeth Cady Stanton died on October 26, 1902, at the age of 87, she was the most famous woman in America. At her pinnacle, she was referred to in the newspaper as "the foremost American woman intellectual of her generation..." who was searching for the "...underlying principles of human and social behavior."

What were her beliefs, her aims? What did she accomplish? In today's terms, as a reformer and public figure, she was first and foremost a feminist. By standards of her day, she was a self-described radical. She became an anti-slavery advocate when the Civil War began. She never wrote a lengthy analytical work. Her aim was to influence opinion towards women. To accomplish this, she turned to oratory and journalism. She became the head of the fight for women's rights first and foremost, and then what came to be called the suffrage movement.

***Editor's Note: I reached out to Ken Burns via his web site, conveyed my mother's anecdote, and asked for clarification about the inspiration for his documentary about Stanton. I received this response: "Dear Greg, Thanks for writing. And we're sorry for your loss. Ken was actually inspired by a biography of Stanton by Elizabeth Griffith—In Her Own Right: The Life of Elizabeth Cady Stanton. Best of luck with everything, Florentine Films"

Elizabeth Cady, her husband Henry Brewster Stanton, and I are descended from our common ancestor, Thomas Stanton, who was married to Katherine Washington, a cousin to George Washington. Their grandson Thomas Stanton was a founder of Stonington, Connecticut. He and his wife Anna Lord had several children, including Hannah, Joseph, and John. It is through these three siblings that we are related. Elizabeth through Hannah; Henry through Joseph; and I through John. Elizabeth and Henry were fifth cousins, and I am a tenth-generation cousin to both.

Theodore Tilton, well-known journalist and Elizabeth Cady Stanton biographer, said in 1897, "I have known you for more than forty years in more than forty characters—suffragist, journalist, lecturer, historian, traveler, prophetess, mater familias, housekeeper, patriot, nurse, baby-tender, cook, milliner-lobbyist, parliamentarian, statistician, legislator, philosopher, tea-pourer, storyteller, satirist, kite flyer, chess player, and theologian."

How did a woman of her day become so renowned? To understand how she became the leader of such a difficult fight at a time when women had no rights, one must look at all of the complex influences and relationships throughout her lifetime. They are many and impossible to discuss at length, but we will cover a few.

Elizabeth Cady was born in 1815 in Johnstown, New York. Her father Daniel Cady worked as a blacksmith. His father James Cady, a farmer, fought in the Revolutionary War and later became a member of the New York State Assembly and the Board of Regents of the State University. Daniel decided to study law. His reputation as an expert on land law was outstanding and, in 1801, allowed him to marry the wealthy Margaret Livingston. He served one term in the House of Representatives and, in 1847, became a justice of the New York State Supreme Court.

By the time Elizabeth was born, her mother Margaret had given birth to six children. Of the six, three had died. In 1826, the only remaining son Eleazer died two months after graduating from college. In 1827, now 42 years old, Margaret gave birth to another son. He died at the age of two. Observing her father's grief over the loss of his sons and his bemoaning the fact that she was not a boy, Elizabeth became determined to equal her brother's achievements.

She displayed an independent streak early in her life, deciding the best path forward was through education, but since no college accepted women, she knew she had to rely on private education.

At her request, the family pastor tutored Elizabeth in Greek, reading to her aloud and discussing the ideas expressed. Her father allowed her to read his law volumes and listen to his conversations with clients. It was here she learned of discrimination against women and, while still a child, tried to cut out all the laws pertaining to women from the law books. Daniel Cady also taught Elizabeth riding and took her with him to Albany as a legal assistant, a most unusual circumstance.

Elizabeth was also influenced by her noted abolitionist cousin, Gerrit Smith. She spent many days at his mansion in Peterboro, N.Y., where she was exposed to ideas about reform, temperance, and abolitionism. Smith's house became a station for the underground railroad, where Elizabeth met many young women fleeing from bondage.

In 1840, she met Henry Stanton, a renowned anti-slavery speaker ten years older than she. He had no money of his own and no prospects of inheritance, but Elizabeth was taken with him and, against the disapproval of her parents, married him a month later, their quick marriage based in part on his promise to take her to the World Anti-Slavery Convention in London. Elizabeth insisted on retaining her own name and adding her husband's to it. She also insisted the word "obey" be eliminated from the marriage ceremony.

It was during her honeymoon in London that Elizabeth met Lucretia Mott and began a relationship that would affect women's history forever. When the women attending the World Anti-Slavery Convention were not allowed to speak, Cady Stanton was so incensed that she proposed to Lucretia that upon their return to the United States, they hold a women's rights convention.

She was pregnant, though, and it would not be until after a period of domestic life and child rearing that her ambitions would begin to be realized. In 1843, the family moved to Boston, where she attended temperance, peace, prison, and anti-slavery reform conventions. Thus, her life of reform began in earnest when she was well into her forties.

Although Susan B. Anthony, Elizabeth's life-long friend and fellow reformer, has held her place in the history of women's suffrage, Stanton never received the credit she should have until recently. She never saw the universal sisterhood of women evolve on a world scale as she hoped.

In later years, Cady was unpopular with many members of the suffrage movement, particularly its younger members, who disagreed with her philosophy. In an organization growing more conservative, Stanton's idea that women's emancipation must be part of the larger political process, not just gain access to the ballot, created a schism in the Suffrage Association.

After two years in office as President, she resigned in 1892, and gave what is considered to be one of the "most eloquent missives of feminism of any period."

Her life as an individual, the people who had influenced her, and the relationships she developed along the way culminated in the following remarks:

"The strongest reason for giving women all the opportunities for higher education, for the full development of her faculties, her forces of mind and body; for giving her the most enlarged freedom of thought and action; a complete emancipation from all forms of bondage, of custom, dependence, superstition; from all the crippling influences of fear—is the solitude and personal responsibility of her own individual life. The strongest reason why we ask for woman a voice in the government under which she lives; in the religion she is asked to believe; equality in social life, where she may earn her bread, is because of her birthright to self-sovereignty; because as an individual, she must rely on herself. No matter how much women prefer to lean, to be protected and supported, nor how much men desire to have them do so, they must make the voyage of life alone, and for safety in an emergency, they must know something of the laws of navigation. To guide our own craft, we must be captain, pilot, engineer; with chart and compass to stand on the wheel; to watch the winds and waves, and know when to take in the sail, and to read the signs in the firmament overall. It matters not whether the solitary voyager is man or woman; nature, having endowed them equally, leaves them to their own skill and judgement in the hour of danger, and, if not equal to the occasion, alike they perish."

We have not yet finished the work that she and her friends started, but thank you, cousin Cady Stanton, for helping to pave the way for the women of the world.

From left, Taylor Jordan, Jacqueline Bachar, and Joanne Hardy.

"Jacqueline spoke to us about her distant cousin Elizabeth Cady Stanton, who was founder of the National Women's Suffrage Association."

NSDAR Cahuilla Chapter Newsletter, 2014, V. 6, #7.

THOMAS LORD m DOROTHY BIRD   THOMAS STANTON m KATHERINE WASHINGTON
ANN LORD   m   THOMAS STANTON

HANNAH STANTON	JOSEPH STANTON	JOHN STANTON
m	m	m
NEHEMIAH PALMER	HANNAH MEAD et al	HANNAH THOMPSON
JOHNATHON PALMER	JOSEPH STANTON	THOMAS STANTON
m	m	m
MERCY MAINWARING	ESTHER GALLOP	ANNA STANTON
PRUDENCE PALMER	JOSEPH STANTON	THOMAS STANTON
m	m	m
EBENEZER CADY	MARY CHAMPLIN	SARAH ------
ELEAZUR CADY	LODOWICK STANTON	JACOB STANTON
m	m	m
TRYPHENA BEEBE	NANCY (THANKFUL) STANTON	JEMIMA WEDGE
DANIEL CADY	JOSEPH STANTON	REBECCA STANTON
m	m	m
MARGARET LIVINGSTON	SUSAN BREWSTER	WILLIAM GOODRICH
ELIZABETH CADY	HENRY BREWSTER STANTON	MARY GOODRICH
m	m	m
HENRY BRESTER STANTON	ELIZABETH CADY	STEPHEN MILLER
BREWSTER		

ERASTUS MILLER
m
MARY JORDAN

STEPHEN E. MILLER
m
EUDORIA TAYLOR

HUGH MILLER
m
LULU SPRAGUE

HERBERT MILLER
m
BERNICE (BARRY) Smith

JACQUELINE MILLER
m
PAUL BACHAR JR

Genealogical Relationship,
Jacqueline Miller Bachar & Elizabeth Cady Stanton

Jacqueline Miller Bachar

Jacqueline Miller Bachar is the editor of *Poetry in The Garden,* an anthology of California women poets, and *Life on The Ohio Frontier: A Collection of Letters from Mary Lott to Deacon John Phillips, 1826-1846;* She is the author of *An Exploration of Boundaries: Art Therapy, Art Education, Psychotherapy; Images of a Woman: A Memoir Journal;* and *La Fête de La Vie (Stories & Poems).*